George A. Thayer

The Braintree Soldiers' Memorial

George A. Thayer

The Braintree Soldiers' Memorial

ISBN/EAN: 9783337308490

Printed in Europe, USA, Canada, Australia, Japan

Cover: Foto ©ninafisch / pixelio.de

More available books at **www.hansebooks.com**

THE

BRAINTREE

SOLDIERS' MEMORIAL:

A RECORD OF THE SERVICES IN THE WAR
OF THE REBELLION

OF THE MEN OF BRAINTREE, MASSACHUSETTS, WHOSE NAMES ARE
INSCRIBED ON THE

BRAINTREE SOLDIERS' MONUMENT;

TOGETHER WITH

APPENDICES CONTAINING A LIST OF BRAINTREE VOLUNTEERS IN THE
UNION ARMY AND NAVY FROM 1861 TO 1865, THE PROCEEDINGS
AT THE DEDICATION OF THE MONUMENT, JUNE 17, 1874,
AND A NOTICE OF THE BRAINTREE BRANCH
OF THE SANITARY COMMISSION.

PREPARED BY

GEORGE A. THAYER.

BOSTON:
ALFRED MUDGE & SON, PRINTERS,
34 School Street.
1877.

THE following record was compiled to be read at the dedication of the Braintree Soldiers' Monument, June 17, 1874.

The compiler has aimed to obtain the full names of the soldiers and of their parents, and to give an accurate account of the term, places, and character of their service; but such thoroughness has, in many cases, been impossible of attainment.

Some of the men were only temporary residents of Braintree at the time of their enlistment, and left no clew to the discovery of any relatives who could furnish information concerning their careers. A very few were substitutes furnished by recruiting brokers of Boston. And of those who were born or long resident in the town previous to their service, it has often been difficult to procure any facts with regard to their families, or any particulars of their army life, other than those supplied in the somewhat scanty public records.

Amid such difficulties it will not be counted strange if omissions of matters worthy of historical preservation should occur in some of the biographies, although much pains has been taken to give the fullest practicable account of each individual's military experience, and the somewhat uncertain and untrustworthy recollections of friends and comrades have, in all possible instances, been compared with and corrected by official documents.

The sources of material for the biographies have been the

records and annual reports of the adjutant-generals of
Massachusetts and other States; a considerable number of
letters, diaries, and clippings from newspapers, kindly furnished by relatives of the men; such regimental and army
histories as would help determine the stations of commands
— and consequently of the members of companies — at
various times; and personal conversation with companions in
arms and home acquaintances of the deceased soldiers.

The names are given in the numerical order of the organi-
zations of the several arms of service, beginning with the artillery, and following with the cavalry, the infantry, and the
navy.

[Note.— The compiler's labors have been much facilitated by assistance
from Messrs. F. A. Hobart, Samuel A. Bates, and Marcus A. Perkins.]

SOLDIERS' MEMORIAL.

FIRST HEAVY ARTILLERY.

ELISHA PAINE GOODNOW, son of Asaph and Maria; enlisted March 3, 1862, in a company which was being recruited in Lynn for the 1st Heavy Artillery (just transformed from the 14th Infantry), and which became Co. M of that regiment. His service was in the fortifications about Washington up to the spring of 1864. After the battle of the Wilderness, the First and several other artillery regiments were organized into a brigade, under General Tyler, and marched to the reinforcement of General Grant's army, reaching the neighborhood of Spotsylvania, on the road from Fredericksburg, on the 19th of May, just as the Confederate General Ewell had attained the road in rear of the Union army for the seizure of its lines of communication. It was the first fight of the artillerists, but the strong brigade, equal in number to an average division of old soldiers, fell upon Ewell with such fury that he was speedily driven back in discomfiture. Swinton, in his "Army of the Potomac," says that "these green battalions, once under fire, displayed an audacity surpassing even the old troops." The 1st Massachusetts lost in the affair 377 men out of its 1,617. Goodnow, foremost in courage, received a shot in his left side, from the effect of which he died in the field in about two hours, and there he was buried. His watch and money, turned over to a comrade to be returned to his widowed mother, were never heard from, let it be hoped rather on account of some subsequent misfortune to that companion than of his intentional dishonesty. Goodnow will be remembered as a fair-faced young man, of somewhat sober look, and of upright character and purpose. He died at the age of twenty-three.

WILLIAM HIGGINS, son of John and Ann, was born in Belfast, Ireland. He enlisted March 17, 1862, in Co. M, 1st Heavy Artillery, at the age of seventeen, and re-enlisted as a veteran on the 20th of March, 1864. As nearly as can be determined, he was with his regiment in its hard service in the Army of the Potomac through the early summer of 1864, was taken prisoner probably on the 22d of June at the Weldon Railroad, when 179 of the regiment were captured, and was sent first to Andersonville, Ga., and thence to Florence, S. C., where he died in prison on the 15th of February, 1865, of malarial fever, contracted in the hideous camp of the prison pen. His age at death was twenty.

TWELFTH BATTERY.

SILAS BINNEY CRANE, son of Joseph and Eliza, was born in Braintree, June —, 1843, and first enlisted in Co. B of the 43d (nine months) Infantry, on the 11th of October, 1862, and was with the company in sundry skirmishes in North Carolina, returning home July 30, 1863. March 26, 1864, he enlisted again as a recruit for the 12th Battery, which was in the Department of the Gulf, where he served for a few weeks, being in some scouts and skirmishes, till he was attacked by the disease which terminated his life in the hospital at Port Hudson, on the 22d of June, 1864. A young man of good principle, he was held in much esteem by the acquaintance whom a natural shyness and reserve allowed him to make.

SECOND CAVALRY.

GEORGE FREDERICK THAYER, son of Ansel and Sarah (Arnold), was born March 29, 1837, and on the 3d of April, 1863, enlisted at San Francisco in the so-called California Battalion of Cavalry, which, being made up largely of Eastern residents on the Pacific coast who were desirous of taking some active part in the war, offered its services to Gov. Andrew, and was incorporated into the 2d Massachusetts Calvary, Colonel Lowell, which left Readville, Mass., on the 11th of May, 1863. He was, with his company, F, in constant service in Maryland and Virginia, near Washington, to the midsummer of 1864, being in several sharp contests with Mosby's men. On the 13th of July, 1864, he, with several comrades, was captured in a fight with a superior force of the enemy, near Rockville, Md., and was carried to Danville, Va., whence, in company with Sergeant Finley, of his regiment, he escaped, on the afternoon of Oct. 20. The narrative of his escape, which he was engaged in writing down to the time of his death, is full of exciting interest, and well exhibits the cool bravery of the man. The two comrades succeeded in removing some boards from an outhouse of the stockade, and, in imminent peril of being shot by the sentinels within and without the prison, hid in the branches of a tree near by, where they stayed until dark, with soldiers and citizens constantly passing beneath their place of refuge. Under cover of the night, they took to the woods, and so marched by night and slept in the woods by day, feeding upon such scanty rations of corn, pigs, or chickens as they might gather from time to time, seldom daring to venture to a house, unless it were to the huts of those trusty friends of the Northern men, the negroes, compelled to wade swamps and creeks, and make long detours through forests and fields to evade the pickets, who were guarding all the main roads and principal towns, and suffering greatly from hunger, cold, wet, and bruised feet. They had no shoes, but only some old socks for foot covering, upon his pair of which Frederick, while in prison, had secretly fastened some thin soles of knapsack leather, using for thread the ravellings from an old shelter tent, and finishing his work with such skill as he treasured from his former trade of a bootmaker. After two hundred and fifty miles of such journeying, they reached the Union Army lines at Newbern, N. C., and thence rejoined their regiment in Virginia. Frederick then received a furlough of twenty days, and visited his Braintree home. Going back to duty in the Shenandoah Valley, on the 1st of January, 1865, he engaged in the arduous cavalry campaign of Sheridan in the early spring, which was conducted through the valley nearly to Lynchburg, and thence eastward to the neighborhood of Richmond, resulting in immense damage to railroads, canals, bridges, and public property generally, and the destruction of many large tobacco warehouses. So trying was the campaign that only three horses of his company were left fit for duty at its end. With a brief rest, the regiment started on the final campaign in pursuit of Lee's army. On the 1st of April, 1865, Sheridan sent his cavalry to seize the important junction of Five Forks, where he hoped to plant his forces across the line of the enemy's retreat and bring him to bay. Frederick was in charge of some led horses in the rear, but requested to be relieved, that he might go to the front and, as he said (recalling his prison sufferings), "get even with the rebels." Thus eager for duty, he was shot through the head and carried senseless to the rear. The papers in his pocket, which would have served for identification of his body, were unfortunately taken from him to be sent home, and so his remains could not be recognized for recovery. He, too, lies buried in Virginia, with only the mark (if he has even that), "Unknown Soldier." His diary, by aid of which his career in 1865 has been followed in compiling this narrative, was kept down to the last night of his life. His twenty-ninth birthday occurred three days before his death. His officers spoke of him as a soldier of sterling character, modest and retiring, but of strong, outspoken principle. To this testimonial those who knew him in civil life will gladly bear witness.

OWEN FOX, Co. H, 2d Cavalry, of Irish birth, was an employee of the Boston Flax Mills, at East Braintree. According to the Adjutant-General's books, he enlisted Oct. 9, 1863, as a recruit, and joined his regiment (probably) Oct. 26, at Vienna, Va. The 2d Cavalry having been organized by one of the most accomplished of regular army officers, Colonel Charles R. Lowell, was constantly called upon for active service against the guerilla bands which infested the vicinity of Washington, and in the spring and early summer of 1864 met with considerable losses in killed, wounded, and prisoners. On the 6th of July a party of about one hundred of the regiment, under Major Forbes, were defeated in an encounter with Mosby's command, and the larger part of them killed or taken prisoners. Fox was in the engagement, and as in the rout the men were flying by different roads at utmost speed, his horse burst a blood-vessel in going down a precipitous descent, and pinned his rider under him. Chaplain Humphreys, from whom information concerning this affair was obtained, was close behind Fox, and with his horse leaped over him as he lay in the road. As the chaplain looked back he heard Fox shout, "I surrender!" and saw Mosby, or one of his men, shoot at him as he galloped past. When, after a few hours' hiding in the woods, the chaplain went back to look after the wounded, he found Fox shot entirely through the abdomen, and with the help of a farmer of the vicinity took him to a neighboring house, where he died at about three o'clock of the morning of the 7th. Fox said that he was shot after he had surrendered, and was extremely indignant at the outrage. He spoke a good deal about his family, and died quietly. While Mr. Humphreys was digging the grave in an adjoining field, a guerilla took him prisoner, and refused him time to finish the burial. The farmer promised to complete the duty, and with this the chaplain was forced to be content. The body of Fox is not unlikely one of that multitude who lie on Arlington Heights, with the inscription, "Unknown Soldier," upon their head-boards. His age at the time of his death was about twenty-four years.

—

THIRD CAVALRY.

John T—— Ayers; born in Maine; was a corporal of Co. C, 4th Massachusetts Militia, and served faithfully at Fortress Monroe and Newport News, from April 22 to July 22, 1861. Aug. 6, 1862, he enlisted with several other men from Braintree in a company which was first attached to the 33d Infantry, was afterwards transferred to the 41st Infantry, and eventually became Co. K, of the 3d Cavalry. His service to June of 1863 was for a time in Virginia, but with no fighting; thence, in the Department of the Gulf, where in all the duties of an infantry soldier in an unhealthy climate, with fatiguing labor of the march, the skirmish, and picket, he gained the highest confidence of his officers and the warm affection of all his companions. In June of 1863 his regiment became the 3d Cavalry, its members having previously been allowed to become mounted riflemen, by providing themselves with horses from the surrounding country. On the 27th of June he was taken prisoner near Baton Rouge, but was exchanged in a few weeks. Thereafter he was steadily with his company on scouts and raids, and in numerous minor or severe fights. He was in the disastrous Red River expedition under General Banks, which began in the late winter of 1864, where the regiment was often sharply engaged and constantly kept in wearisome action, meeting with heavy losses. At the close of this trying campaign in July of 1864, his regiment was converted again into infantry, and sent north to join General Sheridan's command in the Shenandoah Valley of Virginia. Here he became first sergeant of his company. The story of Sheridan's brilliant operations in the fall of 1864 in that valley, which had so often been a valley of humiliation to the Union armies, has been made familiar through the fame in song which has attached to Sheridan's ride from Winchester to the meeting of his somewhat broken army on the 19th of October; how, on Sept. 19, at Opequan Creek, he routed Early's force, with large captures of artillery, battle-flags, and prisoners; how he followed up his success three days after by another assault at Fisher's Hill, taking sixteen guns and many prisoners: and how, on the 19th of October, when the flank of the Union army had been surprised in the morning twilight and the forces driven back disorganized for miles, he rode impetuously on to the field to help turn the tide of disaster into a sweeping victory from which the enemy never rallied in that region, is all well known as one of the most satisfactory series of affairs in the course of the war. Sergeant Ayers was at his post of duty in the battles of Opequan and Fisher's Creek, and when the surprise at Cedar Creek came was prompt in arms only to meet his death. He was struck in the abdomen about eight o'clock in the morning, and though begging to be left on the field, because he declared it useless for his men to try their strength by bearing him off, he was carried to the hospital some miles in the rear, where he died in the course of the afternoon, possibly not before he had heard the glad tidings of victory. His age was about thirty-four. His body was brought to Braintree for burial. The tenderness and respect with which his name is universally mentioned by his comrades, indicate that he was a man worthy to be long remembered as one who lent high honor to the town of his adoption.

JOHN FERDINAND ALBEE, son of John and Susan, was born in Braintree. He enlisted at the age of sixteen as a recruit in Co. K, 3d Cavalry, on the 29th of February. 1864, and saw no active service, his regiment being in the field when he reached New Orleans. While waiting its return he contracted the prevailing disease of the region (chronic diarrhœa), which slew more men than shells or bullets, and died at Morganzia, La., on the 22d of June, 1864. His age was about eighteen.

ELISHA STRONG BOWDITCH, son of John and Ruth G., was born in Braintree, Aug. 18, 1842; enlisted as a recruit in Co. K, 3d Cavalry, on the 7th of December, 1863, and in the following February was at New Orleans. A young man of delicate nurture and little accustomed to hardship, his first experiences of camp life were exceedingly trying to mind and body, and he was, in consequence, an easy victim to the malarious diseases of Louisiana, so that he saw but little active service. He was for a few months with his regiment in its encampment about New Orleans, doing the duty according to his ability, and on the 4th of August was admitted to the barracks hospital of that city, where he died of chronic diarrhœa on the 19th of September, 1864. His letters home are full of evidence of his high-toned principle and very affectionate nature. He was buried in New Orleans.

WILLIAM SANFORD LEACH, son of Elbridge G. and Pauline, was born in New Portland, Me., Aug. 21, 1839. He was a dentist in South Braintree at the time of his enrolment, Aug. 8, 1862 (enlisted in July), in the company with Sergeant Ayers, K, 3d Cavalry. He followed the course of his regiment in its brief Virginia duty and in its operations about New Orleans through the fall and winter of 1862–3. His diary, kept to within two days of his death, contains an intelligent narrative of the life of a volunteer, with all its inconveniences and its ready adaptation to strange conditions, besides giving an interesting view of the scouts and skirmishes of the regiment on its movement towards Port Hudson in the spring of 1863. At the close of that expedition, from which he had suffered greatly through weakness, he was transferred to the Marine Hospital at New Orleans, where, on the night of Aug. 6, 1863, he died so quietly that his comrade in the next bed knew nothing of it till several hours after daylight. From the contents of his diary it is evident that he was a thoughtful and observing as well as conscientious man. His age at time of death was twenty-four (nearly).

EDWARD EVERETT PATTEN, son of Richard S. and Mary J., of South Amesbury, was born March 29, 1836, and was a harness-maker with Warren Mansfield at the time of his enlistment with the Braintree squad of Co. K, 3d Cavalry, on the 8th of August, 1862. Of the fidelity of his service in the Department of the Gulf, all could be said that has been attributed to his other comrades. Constantly with his company, he was ever brave, patient of discomfort, and ready to endure, without murmur, more than his share of duty. He was in the battles of Opequan and Fisher's Hill, in the Shenandoah Valley, and on the 19th of October, 1864, went into the contest of Cedar Creek, though he was so sick that a less couiageous and energetic man would have been in the hospital ; but his place was in the line, and there he received a wound in the left hip, from which he died Nov. 15, 1864, at Newton Barracks Hospital, Baltimore, at the age of twenty-nine (nearly). His conduct was an admirable illustration of the heroic virtues in many a common obscure man, which were brought into conspicuous lustre by the test of war.

ANSEL PENNIMAN THAYER, son of Wm. Franklin and Esther M., enlisted Aug. 6, 1862, in company with Sergeant Ayers and others. He was uniformly with his regiment through the campaigns which have been enumerated. He is reported to have been neither sick nor wounded until the day of his death, which occurred at the battle of Opequan or Winchester, on the 19th of September, 1864, where, in the first fight of the regiment in that vicinity, he was shot through the abdomen, being among the earliest injured. He died in a few hours at the field hospital, at the age of twenty years. The simple but sufficient encomium of his comrades is that he was a *good soldier*.

JOHN FRANCIS WILDE, son of Elisha and Caroline (Healey), was born in Braintree, Dec. 28, 1819, and was in Co. B, 43d (nine months) Infantry, from Oct. 29, 1862, to July 30, 1863. When, during this service, the 44th Massachusetts was besieged in Washington, N. C., he was one of a few who volunteered to carry provisions to them under considerable risk, and was, with the rest, complimented by General Spinola for the skill and bravery shown on this occasion. On the following Dec. 26, 1863, he enlisted as a recruit in Co. K, 3d Cavalry, and was steadily with the regiment, an efficient soldier, until the time of his death. He was engaged in the Red River campaign, and on the 8th

of April, 1864, while the army was in retreat, had a leg
carried away by a shell at Sabine Cross Roads, La., from the
effects of which he very soon died. His intimate companion
attended him until the near approach of the enemy, when he
was left on the field. In March of 1870 the parents of Mr.
Wilde received a note from Merrill Johnson, formerly of the
23d Wisconsin Infantry, announcing that he had in his pos-
session a ring with Wilde's name upon it, which had been
given to him by a rebel prisoner captured the day after the
battle, who said he had taken it from a dead Union soldier,
and this ring his family now have ; it being one which he had
had made when he joined the 43d Regiment, with his name
and residence stamped upon it. Mr. Wilde was forty-four
years old at the time of his last enlistment, and was there-
fore past the age when he would be actuated by mere
impulse ; but he was a man of warm patriotic feeling, and
believed that, having no wife or children, he could better
respond to the needs of the hour than many a younger man.
He had considerable knowledge of the world, acquired
through travel, and much of the handiness which from the
beginning characterized the Massachusetts soldiers, so that he
was often of great service to his comrades in the minor duties
of the camp and march, especially in making them comfort-
able in times of privation or sickness, his experience being
supplemented by a kindly and generous heart. His loss
was sincerely mourned by all who had known him.

GARRETT GEORGE BARRY, son of Richard and Mary, of
Holbrook, enlisted Dec. 13, 1861, at the age of seventeen,
in what was for some time known as the 3d Unattached
Company of Cavalry, Captain Cowen, which was in service
in Louisiana until June of 1863, when it became Co. M, 3d
Massachusetts Cavalry. Notwithstanding his youth, Barry
was soon made a corporal, and for his bravery in an attack

upon the camp of the 4th Mississippi Cavalry, in January of 1863, was presented with one of the trophies of the capture, a fine spy-glass, on which were engraved some words of high commendation from Lieutenant Perkins, his commander. Later, he became a sergeant, and while acting in that capacity at the attack of Sabine Cross Roads, La., in which his last efforts were to keep his men from breaking ranks, in some disorganization, he was shot in the head and instantly killed. A letter received by his parents from his company commander spoke in terms of strong praise concerning his soldierly qualities.

FOURTH CAVALRY.

Alvin Jackson, son of George and Hannah, was born in Readfield, Me., and according to the books of the Adjutant-General, enlisted in Co. H of the 1st Cavalry on the 12th of October, 1861, and was discharged Jan. 10, 1863. Jan. 9, 1864, he enlisted in Co. D of the 4th Cavalry, and was stationed, for the remainder of his service, in South Carolina. The reports of the manner of his death state that on the 15th of January, 1865, he, with several men of his company, was sent with despatches, and the squad, being attacked by the enemy, became divided. Jackson was seen by one of his companions to fall from his horse; and as nothing more was ever heard from him, the presumption is that he was killed. His age was about thirty-eight years.

NINTH INFANTRY.

Cornelius Furfy (or Furphey) was born in Armagh, Ireland, about 1840, and was an employee of the Boston Flax Mills, at East Braintree, when he enlisted in Co. G, 9th

Massachusetts Infantry, on the 11th of June, 1861. His regiment was under McClellan in the peninsular campaign of 1862, being slightly engaged in the affair of Hanover Court House, May 27, and in the engagement near Mechanicsville, June 26, and losing heavily in the battle of Gaines' Mill, June 27, and at Malvern Hill, July 1. In this latter battle, Furfy was mortally wounded. His brother, of the same company, while carrying him to the rear, was also wounded, and compelled to leave his charge upon the field, which was soon occupied by the enemy. His age, at the time of death, was about twenty-two.

TWELFTH REGIMENT.

FRANCIS W. KAHLE, born in Germany, was an operative at Hollingsworth's paper-mill, and was drafted under the call of July, 1863. July 19 he was mustered into Co. C, of the 12th Massachusetts Infantry, at the age of forty, according to the records. He died in the regimental hospital, at Culpepper, Va., of pneumonia, March 6, 1864. His captain, F. B. Pratt, of Weymouth, writes that "he was a good soldier, was always on duty in camp and field, until his last sickness, and was highly esteemed by his comrades." The regiment was engaged in no battle during his service.

TWENTIETH INFANTRY.

THOMAS JOHN CROWELL, son of George and Jane, was born in Horton, Nova Scotia, April 15, 1829, from whence he came to Braintree. He was ardently interested in the anti-slavery cause, and was largely influenced by this zeal in his enlistment. He served in Co. C, 4th Militia, from April

2

to July of 1861, and speedily re-enlisted, joining Co. K, of the 20th Infantry, Aug. 21, 1861, in which he was later a corporal. The 20th was one of the most excellent regiments in the service, and was consequently often placed at dangerous posts. It was involved in the disastrous affair of Ball's Bluff, on the 22d of October, 1861, in which a few Union regiments, attacked by a superior force of the enemy, were compelled to fight with the Potomac River at their backs, and by shooting, drowning, and capture were nearly destroyed. Early in 1862 it joined McClellan's army on the Peninsula, where Crowell participated in an affair with the enemy at West Point, Va., in the battle of Fair Oaks, on the 31st of May, and in the engagement of Nelson's Farm, June 30. The steady picket and fatigue duty of that season, through the mud and swamps of Williamsburg, the Chickahominy, and the White Oak, were a harder trial of the metal of men than even the frequent fighting. Thousands were overcome by this unwonted exposure, and filled the hospitals with sick and the swamps with graves; and the ranks of the 20th were reduced in common with those of other regiments, its men being often without tents and sometimes destitute of blankets. Through this campaign Crowell survived to enter into the great struggle of Antietam, Maryland, Sept. 17, 1862, after whose success for the Union arms he marched to Falmouth, on the banks of the Rappahannock River, where the winter found his regiment confronting Lee's army in Fredericksburg, on the opposite side of the stream. On the 12th of December General Burnside, then commanding the army, proposed to attack Lee, but was prevented from laying one of the pontoon bridges necessary for the crossing by the annoying fire of rebel sharpshooters, who were secreted in the brick houses of Fredericksburg. The task of clearing the way of these sharpshooters was assigned to Hall's Brigade, to which the 20th belonged, and passing the river in small boats they, by

19

a gallant surprise, accomplished the work; but the enemy,
reinforced, soon rallied in one of the main streets, which
ran parallel to the Rappahannock, from which the 20th was
ordered to dislodge them. In column by company it marched
up the street, with musketry pouring upon it on every side,
from cellar and garret, but not flinching till it had attained
its purpose. Crowell escaped all injury here; but the next
afternoon, the 13th, the brigade was ordered to the still more
formidable work of attacking rifle-pits, held by a strong line
of infantry and covered by numerous artillery. On the
double-quick they moved to their duty, met by tremendous
volleys of musketry and a storm of canister and shell, till
human nature could bear no more, and they fell back under
cover. Only *four* of Co. K were left, and Crowell was not
of these. In a few hours he crawled into his regimental
lines with a mortal wound in his left breast near the heart,
and with another bullet in his thigh. That night he died in
hospital, conscious and cheerful, his last words being of his
family. "Tell them," he said, "that they have the consola-
tion of knowing that my life was offered for the good of the
country." Lieutenant Ropes, commanding the company,
spoke of his behaving in the fight "with his usual intrepid-
ity"; and Sergeant Clark said, "He was always in his place,
and brave as a lion." No man ever more completely vindi-
cated his political principles by heroic deeds and death than
did Corporal Crowell.

TWENTY-SECOND INFANTRY.

Three men from Braintree, in this regiment, lost their lives
in the same battle, viz., Crickmay, Fogg, and Dalton.

CHARLES HENRY CRICKMAY, son of Robert and Elizabeth,
of England, enlisted at the age of thirty-four in the Quincy

Co. II, of the 4th Militia (the company from Braintree being full), and served from April to July of 1861. On the 6th of September, 1861, he enlisted in Co. I, of the 22d Infantry, then called Senator Wilson's regiment, and with it joined McClellan's army on the Peninsula. He saw no fighting of consequence till the 27th of June, 1862, when occurred the severe battle of Gaines' Mill, in which 70,000 Confederates under Stonewall Jackson attacked 30,000 Union troops, and threw back in disaster the right flank of McClellan's army. The 22d lost very heavily here, and with the rest of the Union regiments left its killed and wounded in the enemy's hands. Crickmay was wounded in the thigh, and being taken to Richmond, underwent an amputation, from which he died June 30, 1862. He was a brave man, of generous impulses. He had the rank of corporal. His body was never recovered.

ALEXANDER RESHAW FOGG, son of Seth and Betsy, of Denmark, Maine, also enlisted in Co. I, of the 22d, on the 15th of September, 1861, as a teamster, but was afterwards transferred to the ranks. He was one of the wounded at Gaines' Mills, and was undoubtedly buried by the enemy. His age was thirty-nine. His body was not recovered.

JEREMIAH DALTON, 2D, son of Tristam and Ann, was in Co. G, Fifth Militia, which was in the first battle of Bull Run, his service being from May 1 to July 31, 1861. He enlisted again Oct. 1, 1861, in Co. E of the 22d, was made a corporal, and was killed at Gaines' Mill, June 27, 1862, at the age of twenty-one. His body was left on the field.

TWENTY-FOURTH INFANTRY.

DANIEL AUSTIN THAYER, son of Gideon and Sarah H.,
at the age of twenty-three enlisted, July 28, 1862, from
Gloucester, in Co. C of the 24th Infantry, and died of
chronic diarrhœa in hospital at Hilton Head, S. C., Jan. 4,
1864. His regiment was, during the time when he belonged
to it, with General Gilmore at Morris Island, near Charleston,
protecting the siege operations.

WILLIAM MARTIN HARMON, son of William and Hannah,
enlisted on the 13th of November, 1861, at the age of
eighteen, in Co. G, 24th Massachusetts Infantry. He was
with the regiment in the battle of Roanoke Island, in February, 1862, one of the first Union successes, in which
Burnside captured some 1,500 prisoners; was at the battle
near Newbern, N. C., on the following 14th of March, and
thence in sundry affairs at Washington, N. C., at Kingston,
and at Whitehall. He left his regiment in the spring of
1863, and died in hospital at Newbern, of chronic diarrhœa,
April 30, 1863.

TWENTY-EIGHTH INFANTRY.

LAWRENCE MCLAUGHLIN, born in Ireland, was a resident
of Braintree, and in the latter part of 1861, at the age of
eighteen, enlisted in Co. I, 28th Infantry. He re-enlisted
as a veteran Jan. 1, 1864. His friends state that he was
steadily with his regiment from his enrolment to the day of
his death, with the exception of a three days' absence, on
account of a wound in the head, and a short furlough in the
winter of 1863, which he passed in Braintree. The 28th
had a varied experience. It was, at first, on duty in South

Carolina, having left Massachusetts Jan. 11, 1862; was in several skirmishes there, and in an attack upon Fort Johnson; thence in Virginia, was at the second battle of Bull Run, with considerable loss, and at Chantilly; was active at Antietam; suffered at Fredericksburg; was slightly engaged at Chancellorsville, and heavily again at Gettysburg; was conspicuous in Meade's campaign of Mine Run, in the fall of 1863; and in 1864 was in the battles of the Wilderness, of Spotsylvania, of Cold Harbor, and in the siege of Petersburg. On the 22d of June, after McLaughlin had passed unhurt through a sharp skirmish with the enemy, he was sent on picket in the evening, and was soon shot dead. His body was not recovered.

CHARLES GRAY was probably a substitute, and not a resident of the town, at the time of his enlistment. The slight facts known about him are drawn from the Adjutant-General's records. He enlisted in Co. D, 28th Infantry, Aug. 10, 1863, and died in a Southern prison Sept. 15, 1864. The career of his regiment has been mentioned in connection with McLaughlin's name. In all likelihood, Gray was captured in one of the battles under General Grant in the summer of 1864.

AMOS ATKINS LORING, Co. B, 28th Infantry, son of Benjamin J. and Elizabeth, enlisted Jan. 5, 1864, at the age of eighteen, was made a drummer, and died of disease at City Point, Virginia, at a date unknown.

THIRTY-SECOND INFANTRY.

First Sergeant LORING WINTHROP THAYER, son of Ansel and Sarah (Arnold), was a member of Co. C, of the 4th

Massachusetts Militia, and served with his regiment at
Fortress Monroe and Newport News, Va., from April to
July of 1861. In December of that year he enlisted again
in the company raised by Captain C. C. Bumpus, which, for
a time, was in garrison at Fort Warren until it became Co. E,
of the 32d Infantry, — a three years' regiment, — and was
ordered to Washington in May, 1862. On the 3d of July,
the regiment joined McClellan's army at Harrison's Landing,
on James River. From that time forward, Sergeant Thayer
was constantly with his regiment in active service, never
absent from sickness nor receiving any wounds till the day
of his death. He was, with his company, in reserve at
Chantilly and Antietam in September, and was engaged at
Fredericksburg in December of 1862. In the following
spring, he was in the campaign of Chancellorsville, and in
July of 1863 at Gettysburg, where his regiment met with
heavy loss. The severe fall and winter campaign of General
Meade at Mine Run and on the line of the Orange and
Alexandria Railroad tried the endurance of the regiment as
well as proved Sergeant Thayer's faithfulness. When Grant
began the march upon Richmond in the spring of 1864,
which was to result in the long list of terrible battles and of
picket skirmishes almost as deadly as battles, which was
not to end until the surrender of Lee, the 32d entered
upon the active duties of the field, losing heavily in
the Wilderness, being under constant vigilance at Spotsylvania, then slightly engaged at the North Anna River, and
again and again at Mechanicsville, at Bethesda Church, and
at Petersburg and the Weldon Railroad. So wasting was
this summer upon the regiment, that the 30th of September
found Sergeant Thayer in command of his company, which
was without a commissioned officer when it was ordered to
an assault upon Fort McRae, of the Petersburg line, where,
in what is variously known as the affair of Peebles Farm or
Poplar Grove Church, he received the fatal shot. A warm,

sympathetic letter from his surviving company comrades, sent to his parents under date of Oct. 20, 1864, testified to his great popularity as an associate and to his high, soldierly qualities. He was thoroughly brave and nobly patriotic. He re-enlisted for three years in January of 1864, and on his return from furlough received his promotion from sergeant to first sergeant. His old company commander bears witness that "he was one of the best men in the service, — trusty, faithful to all orders, and brave to a fault." His age at death was twenty-four.

LEONARD F. HUFF, son of Benjamin and ——, at the age of twenty-one enlisted in Co. E, 32d Infantry, Dec. 2, 1861, and after a short service in the forts of Boston Harbor, went with his regiment, in the summer of 1862, to McClellan's army, which had just passed through its seven days' battles on the Virginia peninsula. While lying at Harrison's Landing, on the James River, he was attacked with disease, and was sent to hospital at Philadelphia, where he died, Aug. 23, 1862. His comrades report him to have been an exemplary soldier.

HENRY T. WADE, parentage not ascertained, enlisted at the age of twenty-seven, in Co. E, 32d Infantry, on the 25th of November, 1861, was mustered Dec. 2, 1861, and was killed at the battle of Gettysburg, July 2, 1863. His regiment was active in the battle of Fredericksburg, was slightly engaged at Chancellorsville, and lost heavily at Gettysburg, where he died.

ANTHONY COLUMBUS, who was probably a substitute, appears to have enlisted in Co. K of the 9th Regiment, Aug. 22, 1863, and when that regiment was mustered out of service was, with other men whose terms were unexpired, transferred to Co. I of the 32d Infantry, of which he was a member when he died, at time and place unknown.

THIRTY-THIRD INFANTRY.

First Lieutenant and Brevet-Captain Edgar Lewis Bumpus, son of Cephas C. and Amelia D., born in North Bridgewater, Jan. 18, 1838, was a member of his father's company, C, of the 4th Militia, in 1861, and while his regiment was lying at Newport News, Va., in June, was one of two or three men who, desirous of varying the monotony of camp life, volunteered to join the troops which were going to Big Bethel, where his clothes were perforated by a bullet. On the 13th of the September following his return he joined McPherson's company of United States Sappers and Miners at Fort Independence, Boston Harbor, from which he was discharged for disability, May 16, 1862. He again enlisted, Aug. 5, 1862, in Co. A, 33d Massachusetts Infantry, and was mustered as corporal, but in a few weeks became sergeant, and was transferred to Co. E. He was commissioned as second lieutenant, June 20, 1863, as first lieutenant, March 9, 1864, and, after his death, had his merit recognized by a brevet of captain, dated May 22, 1865. To the fall of 1863 the 33d Regiment was in Virginia, in the 11th Corps, but was not involved in the rout at Chancellorsville, which gave that corps such a bad name. It was one of a few picked regiments sent to support the cavalry at the contest of Beverly Ford on the 9th of June, 1863, and was in the most fearful. and exposed part of the battle-field of Gettysburg, July 3, at Cemetery Hill, where for three hours one hundred and fifty-five Confederate guns rained a storm of shot and shell, largely concentrated upon this key-point of the field. In both of these affairs Bumpus was the color-sergeant, the well-known position of honor and of imminent danger. In the fall of 1863, the 33d was sent under General Hooker to Rosecrans' Army of the Cumberland, and on the 28th of

October was engaged in a brave and victorious midnight assault upon a division of the enemy near the base of Lookout Mountain, at Wauhatchie. At the opening of Sherman's campaign against Atlanta, in the spring of 1864, the regiment was in Butterfield's third division of the 20th Corps, but had no engagement till the battle of Resaca, Ga., on Sunday, May 15, when it was ordered to assault the enemy's works upon a hill strongly protected by *abattis* and underbrush. Bumpus was temporarily in command of the color company, as first lieutenant, and while his command was in some slight confusion, owing to difficulties of manœuvring, he stepped before them with the encouragement, " Boys, stand by your colors ! " and was almost immediately shot through the head. His age was twenty-four. His remains lie in the National Cemetery at Chattanooga. The writer of this account frequently saw him in the spring of his death, and talked with him but a few hours before his last fight. He was uniformly in good spirits and imbued with a right patriotism. The excellence of his standing in his regiment is testified to by the nature of the duties and honors so many times laid upon him. His loss was profoundly regretted in his regiment by men who had known his fidelity in many a trying responsibility, and was sorrowed over by many at home besides his kindred who remembered him as an earnest, generous, and high-minded young man.

TIMOTHY HORACE CAIN, son of Rhodes and Louisa (Holbrook), joined Co. K of the 33d Infantry at the time of its formation, Aug. 8, 1862, and followed the career of that regiment through Virginia, at Gettysburg, at Lookout Mountain, at Resaca, and as far towards Atlanta as the battle of Dallas, on the 25th of May, 1864, where he was slightly wounded. Being sent to hospital at Louisville, Ky., he never returned to his company, but died a year later at Alexandria, Va., July 7, 1865, of chronic diarrhœa. Down to the time of his wound he was never reported absent, and always bore the reputation of a good soldier. His reported age at enlistment was twenty-one.

THIRTY-SIXTH INFANTRY.

DANIEL W. DEAN, at the age of nineteen, enlisted Aug. 8, 1862, in Co. K, 36th Infantry, and is reported to have died in the same year, probably from disease.

SETH DEAN, possibly a brother of the above, at the age of twenty-four enlisted in the same company, under the same date, and died at Windmill Point Hospital, Va., near Acquia Creek, Jan. 27, 1863. Concerning the identity and origin of these men, there is some uncertainty. A Seth Dean was in Co. A, 1st Battalion Heavy Artillery, and was discharged for disability July 20, 1862. Perhaps they were the same, though the records of age differ by ten years.

THIRTY-EIGHTH INFANTRY.

EDWARD DAVID, son of Lyman and Lavinia, of Venice, N. Y., was enrolled August 13, 1862, in Co. K of the 38th Infantry, and was killed June 14, 1863, at Port Hudson, La. His regiment was in the 19th Corps, Emery's Division, General Banks's army. It was engaged in an affair with the enemy at Fort Bisland, in the Teche country, where it met with some loss, and was in the siege of Port Hudson. The brigade to which it belonged made an ineffectual assault upon some rebel works at the latter place, on the 14th of June, and was compelled to lie under cover of bushes and earthworks until darkness should enable it to retreat. Edward, leaving his equipments, took a canteen to go to the rear for water, determined to run the risk for his pressing need, and was never again seen by his brother Solon, who was in the company with him. The Pioneer Corps described one like him who was shot through the head while going for water, and his fate was thus pretty conclusively established. His body was not recovered. Old associates remember him as a pleasant and amiable young man.

THIRTY-NINTH INFANTRY.

JAMES BANNON, born in Ireland, enlisted in Co. G, 39th Infantry, in August or September (Sept. 2, Adjutant-General's records), 1862, at the age of thirty-eight. The first battles of the regiment were in Grant's campaign of 1864, where its losses were small, until it reached Petersburg. Bannon was, however, slightly wounded in the battle of the Wilderness, but continued in the field. At the battle of Weldon Railroad, on the 19th of August, 1864, nearly the whole of the 39th was captured, and Bannon, among them, was taken to Salisbury Prison, where he remained six months, being released in February, 1865. The hardships of the prison wore greatly upon him, although the severity of the confinement was mitigated by his being assigned to duty in the hospital cook-house of the prison. His death, which occurred at his home in Braintree on the 27th of March, 1865, was accelerated by the prison experience, together with the accidental use of some poisonous medicine in the hospital after his release.

FORTY-SECOND INFANTRY (100 DAYS).

HENRY WINSLOW DEAN, son of Horatio and Melinda, was born in Braintree, May 4, 1832, and was in Co. C of the 4th Militia from April to July of 1861. July 19, 1864, he joined the company of one hundred days' men from Braintree, which was assigned to the 42d Regiment, and did duty in the fortifications of Washington. He died in Sickles s Barracks Hospital, Alexandria, of chronic diarrhœa, Oct. 9, 1864. Although by no means strong at the time of his enlistment, he was eager to be with his old associates and do his part of the required service.

SECOND LOUISIANA (COLORED) INFANTRY.

EBENEZER CODDINGTON THAYER, JR., son of Ebenezer C. and Sarah Jackson, at the age of twenty-four enlisted in Co. K of the 31st Massachusetts Infantry, under date of Jan. 29, 1862, and became a corporal. His regiment was in the Department of the Gulf, when General Butler gave him the warrant of sergeant-major of the 2d Louisiana Colored Infantry, in which he was subsequently commissioned as second lieutenant. He served in the siege of Port Hudson and in the Red River expedition, during the last part of which he was wounded in the left lung while, as acting adjutant, he was quelling a disturbance among some of his soldiers. He died from hemorrhage in the St. James Hospital at New Orleans on the 14th of April, 1864. After his body had laid embalmed in the undertaker's rooms for more than a year, it was sent North, and lies in the cemetery at Braintree. His familiar neighbors speak of him as a young man of uncommonly high character.

THIRD MARYLAND INFANTRY.

JOHN FINNIGAN, son of James and Catherine, was a member of Co. C, 4th Militia, from April to July 22, 1861. In February of 1862, persons representing themselves as recruiting officers for Maryland regiments persuaded thirty or forty men from Massachusetts to go with them to Maryland, and there left them to shift for themselves. Finnigan among these, with one or two other Braintree men, enrolled himself in the 3d Maryland Infantry, which eventually belonged to the 2d Brigade, 2d division of the 12th Corps. He died of chronic diarrhœa in the regimental hospital of Acquia Landing, March 12, 1863, at the age of twenty. A letter from his captain (Charles G. Downs, Co. B) says he had been complaining for six months.

TWENTY-FIFTH NEW YORK INFANTRY.

THOMAS SMITH, corporal of Co. II, enlisted May 13, 1861, in this regiment, under Colonel James E. Kerrigan. He is reported to have been wounded in the affair of Hanover Court House, May 27, 1862, and to have died a few weeks later near Gaines' Mill, Virginia.

SEVENTIETH NEW YORK.

In the summer of 1861, when the general government was undecided concerning its powers of raising troops, and seemed little to appreciate the magnitude of the impending danger, the raising of more than six regiments was discouraged in Massachusetts, despite Governor Andrew's vigorous protest, so that some companies, already formed, received permission to join New York regiments. To one of these companies belonged three men from Braintree, two Bunkers and Parker, who were assigned to the so-called Mozart Brigade under Daniel Sickles, then being organized at Staten Island, New York.

Levi Bunker, son of Nahum and Irene, born Jan. 1, 1840, enlisted June 20, 1861, in Captain Bugbee's company, which became a part of Colonel Wm. Dwight Jr.'s regiment, the Seventieth New York, of Sickles's Brigade. He was guarding the Lower Potomac until May, of 1862, when he joined McClellan on the Peninsula, and on the 5th of that month was engaged in the severe battle of Williamsburgh, where he was taken prisoner. His confinement was short, but he had a taste of the hard treatment and low diet with which unhappy prisoners afterward became sadly familar, for he spoke of his food for the three days' march to Richmond as being a pint of meal each day, cooked in the ashes. When released he came home on furlough, and returned to join in the battle of Fredericksburg in December, 1862, and of Chancellorsville in May, 1863, where, through extreme exposure and exhaustion, he contracted the disease from which he died at Washington, June 16, 1863, at the age of twenty-three years. His body is in the soldiers' cemetery at Arlington Heights, Virginia.

Edward Silas Bunker, brother of Levi, born Oct. 13, 1844, enlisted July 13, 1861, in the same company and regiment. He lost his shoes in the mud, the night before Williamsburg, and so fought barefoot all day through the rain, and was wounded in the left arm and taken prisoner, his wound not being dressed for three days. This undue exposure and privation planted the seeds of the fever of which he died at home, while on furlough, Sept. 11, 1862. He is buried in South Braintree.

ALFRED EMMONS PARKER, a cousin of the Bunkers, son of Thomas and Esther, born Oct. 21, 1842, enlisted July 15, 1861, in the same company and regiment with his cousins, and was mortally wounded on the 5th of May, 1862, at the battle of Williamsburg, in which his captain was killed and his colonel was dangerously wounded. His cousin was allowed to bear him to the rear, but soon left him, and the place of his burial is unknown.

These young men were all of excellent habits and character.

EIGHTH VERMONT INFANTRY.

BENJAMIN FRANKLIN ARNOLD, son of Benjamin and Rebecca, was born in Randolph, Mass., March 30, 1836, and enlisted from Randolph, Vt., where he was temporarily residing, in Co. F, of the 12th Vermont, a nine months' regiment. He was enrolled Oct. 4, 1862, and was mustered out July 21, 1863. In the following December (23), he enlisted in the 8th Vermont, a three years' regiment, and was mustered Jan. 6, 1864, and was with his regiment in the Gulf Department till its transfer to the Shenandoah Valley, with the 19th Corps, in the summer of 1864. On the march through Maryland he received a sunstroke, which kept him in the hospital at Baltimore a few weeks, but he rejoined the regiment in the valley, where he was taken prisoner on the morning of the battle of Cedar Creek, Oct. 19, 1864, while venturing on a foraging expedition too far into the enemy's lines. He died in Salisbury Prison, Dec. 29, 1864, one of that great company of martyrs who met the most cruel of deaths in the war.

SEVENTEENTH VERMONT.

NELSON ARNOLD, son of Benjamin and Rebecca, born in
Randolph, Sept. 5, 1840, was also a resident of Randolph,
Vt., when, with his brother, he joined the nine months'
12th Vermont Infantry, Co. F, Oct. 18, 1862. On the 29th
of September, 1863, he was enrolled in Co. D, 17th Vermont, and entered the 9th Corps. His regiment was actively
engaged with this corps of General Burnside's in the battles of
1864, under General Grant, losing steadily; but Arnold is
reported to have been uninjured down to the time when he
was placed in the dangerous works before Petersburg, where,
on the 19th of June, 1864, he was shot through the head by
a sharp-shooter. He was buried in Virginia.

NAVY.

PAUL NADELL enlisted, at the age of thirty, in Co. C, 14th
Mass. Infantry, on the 5th of July, 1861, and served creditably after its change to artillery. He re-enlisted as a veteran
Feb. 1, 1864, and was discharged for transfer to the United
States Navy on the 13th of April, 1864. He died in this
arm of the service, at a date not ascertained. A lieutenant
of his company of artillery praises him as having been a
prompt and reliable soldier.

NOTE.—The name of Richard Furfy, 9th Infantry, appears upon the
Soldiers' Monument as killed in battle. Furfy was *not* killed, though the
printed register of the adjutant-general of Massachusetts so declares,
but was only wounded in the battle of the Wilderness, in May, 1864, and
was mustered out of service in Boston, June 21, 1864. These facts the
writer had from Furfy's own lips.

APPENDIX I.

A LIST OF OFFICERS AND ENLISTED MEN OF UNITED STATES
VOLUNTEERS FROM BRAINTREE, IN THE YEARS 1861 TO 1865.

THIS list is mainly drawn from the printed records of the Massachusetts Adjutant-General's office, corrected by a record of the men
accredited to the quota of the town, kept by Elias Hayward, Esq.,
formerly town clerk.

It cannot claim to be free from errors or omissions. Many names
are variously spelled in the public registers, and not improbably some
enlistments in regiments out of the State are unrecorded in either of
the above-mentioned official lists.

The men of the three years' regiments are mentioned first, the
officers being placed in order of rank and seniority of commission; and
where service has been performed in several commands, the names are
repeated.

COMMISSIONED OFFICERS.

THREE YEARS' REGIMENTS.

Warren M. Babbitt, Surgeon 103d U. S. Colored Troops, March 7, 1865; Assistant
Surgeon 55th Mass. Infantry, Aug. 11, 1863. Mustered out, April 30, 1866.

Cephas C. Bumpus, Captain 32d Infantry, Dec. 7, 1861, to April 20, 1863; Captain
3d Heavy Artillery, Sept. 1, 1863, to Jan. 16, 1865.

George A. Thayer, Captain 2d Infantry, July 26, 1863, to July 14, 1865; 1st
Lieutenant, March 30, 1863; 2d Lieutenant, Oct. 16, 1862.

Norman F. Steele, Captain 32d Infantry, Sept. 29, 1863, to Dec. 5, 1864; 1st
Lieutenant, Oct. 21, 1862; 2d Lieutenant, Aug. 14, 1862.

Edgar L. Bumpus, Brevet-Captain 33d Infantry, May 22, 1865; 1st Lieutenant,
March 9, 1864; 2d Lieutenant, June 20, 1863. Killed in battle, May 15, 1864.

Everett C. Bumpus, 1st Lieutenant 3d Heavy Artillery, Oct. 28, 1864, to Sept. 18,
1865; 2d Lieutenant, Sept. 1, 1863.

Edward H. Mellus, 1st Lieutenant 3d Heavy Artillery, June 13, 1865, to Sept. 18,
1865; 2d Lieutenant, May 28, 1864.

Richard M. Sanborn, 1st Lieutenant 3d Cavalry (complimentary), to date from
Oct. 5, 1865; 2d Lieutenant, from Aug. 17, 1865. Mustered out as 1st Sergeant,
Sept. 28, 1865.
Theodore C. Howe, 1st Lieutenant 3d Cavalry (complimentary), to date from
Oct. 5, 1865. Mustered out as Quartermaster-Sergeant, Sept. 28, 1865.
James B. Leonard, 2d Lieutenant 32d Infantry, Nov. 29, 1862, to Jan. 1, 1863.
Ebenezer C. Thayer, Jr., 2d Lieutenant 2d Louisiana Infantry, from ——.
Died, April 14, 1864.
Marcus M. Pool, 2d Lieutenant 1st Heavy Artillery, Oct. 6, 1864, to May 15, 1865.

COMMISSIONED OFFICERS.

VOLUNTEER MILITIA.

Cephas C. Bumpus, Captain Co. C, 4th Infantry (3 months), April 22 to July 22,
1861.
James T. Stevens, Captain Co. I, 42d Infantry (100 days), July 19 to Nov. 11, 1864;
1st Lieutenant Co. C, 4th Infantry, April 22 to July 22, 1861.
Isaac P. Fuller, 2d Lieutenant Co. C, 4th Infantry, April 22 to July 22, 1861.
John C. Sanborn, 2d Lieutenant Co. B, 43d Infantry (9 months), Oct. 11, 1862, to
July 30, 1863.
Charles A. Arnold, 2d Lieutenant Co. I, 42d Infantry (100 days), July 19 to
Nov. 11, 1864.

ENLISTED MEN.

N. B. — Where the name of a soldier is followed by the name of some other
town than Braintree, it is to be understood that such town eventually claimed the
man as properly belonging to it.

*Co. C, 4th M. V. M., from April 22 to
July 22, 1861.*

Wm. M. Richards, 1st Sergeant.
Joseph L. Frazier, Sergeant.
Andrew G. King, Sergeant.
Edgar L. Bumpus, Sergeant.
Samuel M. Hollis, Corporal.
Reuben F. Hollis, Corporal.
John T. Ayers, Corporal.
John C. Sanborn, Corporal.
Charles A. Arnold.
Marcus P. Arnold
James T. Bestick.
John E. Boyle.
Everett C. Bumpus.
Jno. R. Carmichael.
Jno. Coughlan.
Chandler Cox.
Nelson Cox.
Marcus F. Cram.
Thomas J. Crowell.
Wm. Cunningham.
Wm. A. Daggett.

Solon David.
Henry W. Dean.
James Donahoe.
Peter Donahoe.
Lawrence A. Dyer.
Alphons Field.
John Finnegan.
Roland E. Foster.
Wm. B. Foster.
Nathan T. Freeman.
Henry W. Gammons.
Charles Gifford.
Joseph E. Holbrook.
George F. Howard.
Thomas Houston.
Leonard F. Jones.
James B. Leonard.
Wm. Leggett.
Thomas J. Morton.
Edward H. Mellus.
Francis McConity.
Wm. H. McGann.
Albert S Nason.
Marcus A. Perkins.

4th. Co. C (continued).

Henry H. Shedd.
Norman F. Steele.
Thomas B. Stoddard.
Elihu M. Thayer.
Joseph P. Thayer.
Loring W. Thayer.
Andrew Toomey.
Henry W. Wright.

4th. Co. H.

Chas. H. Crickmay.!

5th. Co. G.

Jeremiah Dalton, Jr., May 1 to July 31, 1861.

42d, 100 days, from July 14 to Nov. 11, 1864.

Co. A.

Edward A. Fisher, Corporal.

Co. I.

Cranmore N. Wallace, 1st Sergeant.
John R. Carmichael, Sergeant.
1. P. Fuller, Sergeant.
Robert Gillespie, Sergeant.
Wm. L. Pratt, Corporal.
Francis A Wallace, Corporal.
Marcus A. Perkins, Corporal.
George W. Abbott.
J. Fred Allen.
Fred C. Armstrong.
B. Herbert Bartlett.
Henry W. Dean (to Sept. 21, '64).
Otis B. Dean.
Edwin F. French.
Wm. L. Gage.
Caleb H. Hayden.
Charles T. Hayden.
Lorenzo Hayden.
Waldo Holbrook
Walter Holbrook.
Davis W. Howard.
Moses Hunt, 2d.
Moses N. Hunt.
Newell A. Langley.
John McDermott.
Ruel B. Moody.
George W. Nickerson.
Henry Pratt.
Samuel Rennie.
Charles R. Smith.
Thomas O. Sullivan.
Francis P. Thayer.
Lucian M. Thayer.
Fred H. Wales.
George D. Willis.
James M. Willis.

20th Unattached Co.

Nelson Beals, Aug. 11, to Nov. 18, 1864.

43d, 9 months, from Oct. 11,1862, to July 30, 1863.

Co. B.

Edward H. Mellus, Sergeant
Charles W. Bean, Corporal.
Charles A. Arnold, Corporal.
Thomas B. Stoddard, Corporal.
Jonathan R. Clark, Corporal.
Hiram E. Abbott.
John R. Carmichael.
Silas B. Crane.
Robert M. Cummings.
Wm. B. Denton.
Edward A. Fisher.
Hosea B. Hayden.
Hosea B. Hayden, 2d.
Wm. G. Hill.
Albert O. Hollis.
George A. Howe.
Charles B. Leonard.
George A. Mower.
Wm. W. Mower.
Shubael M. Norton.
John F. Pool.
Jacob C. Snow.
Cranmore N. Wallace.
Frank Wallace.
John F. Wild.
Morrill Williams.

44th. Co. H.

Everett C. Bumpus, Sept. 12, 1862, to June 18, 1863.

Co. I.

Joseph H. J. Thayer, Sept. 12, 1862, to June 18, 1863.

45th. Co. A.

John W. Fowle, Musician, Oct. 13, 1862, to July 7, 1863.

47th. Co. K.

James Willis, Oct. 31, 1862, to Sept. 1, 1863.
John Wilson, Oct. 31, 1862, to Sept. 1, 1863.

48th. Co. I.

John Freel, Corporal, Oct. 18, 1862, to Sept. 3, 1863.

Co. K.

James Dooley, Nov. 1, 1862, to Sept. 3, 1863.

MASS. VOLUNTEERS, THREE YEARS.

2d Battery Light Artillery.

Wm. E. Foye, Sept. 3, 1864, to June 11, 1865.

7th Battery.

John Brennon, Jan. 1, 1864, to Nov. 10, 1865.

38

12th Battery.

Silas B. Crane, March 26, 1864. Died at Port Hudson, June 22, 1864.

1st Heavy Artillery. Co. C.

Paul Nadell, July 5, 1861, to Jan. 31, 1864. Re-enlisted Feb. 1, 1864. Transferred to navy, April 13, 1864. Died.
Marcus M. Pool, July 5, 1861, to Dec. 21, 1863; Sergeant; re-enlisted Dec. 22, 1863. (See Commissioned Officers.)
James E. Hobart, July 5, 1861. Re-enlisted Dec. 6, 1863, to Aug. 16, 1865.

Co. E.

James T. Bestick, Sergeant, Aug. 6, 1862, to March 26, 1865.
Calvin Briggs, Aug. 6, 1862. Transferred to Veteran Reserve Corps, July 25, 1863.
Edward S. Dean, Aug. 6, 1862, to July 8, 1864.
Henry W. Gammons, Aug. 6, 1862. Discharged, July 8, 1864. (See 2d Cavalry.)

Co. I.

John F. Salmon, July 5, 1861, to July 8, 1864.

Co. M.

Linus C. Bird, March 3, 1862, to March 10, 1864. Re-enlisted March 10, 1864. Transferred to Veteran Reserve Corps, Oct. 1, 1864.
Dennis Foley, March 6, 1862. Re-enlisted (Weymouth), March 21, 1864, to Aug. 16, 1865.
Elisha P. Goodnow, March 3, 1862. Re-enlisted March 10, 1864. Killed May 19, 1864.
Wm. Higgins, March 17, 1862. Re-enlisted March 21, 1864. Died Feb. 15, 1865.
Michael McDonald, March 6, 1862, to March 6, 1865.

2d Heavy Artillery. Co. C.

John E. Boyle, Sept. 5, 1864. Transferred Jan. 9, 1865, to 17th Infantry. Discharged June 26, 1865.
Nehemiah T. Dyer, Sept. 5, 1864, to June 26, 1865.
George P. Hollis, Sept. 5, 1864, to June 26, 1865. Transferred to Co. L, Jan. 13, 1865.
Albert T. Pool, Sept. 5, 1864. Transferred, Jan. 9, 1865, to 17th Infantry. Discharged June 30, 1865.
Andrew C. Toomey, Sept. 5, 1864. Transferred, Jan. 9, 1865, to 17th Infantry. Discharged June 30, 1865.

Co. F.

Fred W. Ingraham, Sergeant, Sept. 5, 1864, to June 26, 1865.
George Atwell, Sept. 5, 1864. Transferred, Jan. 17, 1865, to 17th Infantry.

John Shanley, Aug. 29, 1864. Died Dec 29, 1864. (North Bridgewater.)
Hiram S. Thayer, Sept. 5, 1864, to June 26, 1865.

Co. G.

John Navan, Aug. 29, 1864. Transferred, Dec. 16, 1864, to 17th Infantry. Discharged June 30, 1865.

Co. H.

Samuel Meeker, Aug. 9, 1864, to Sept. 3, 1865.

Co. L.

Edward Freel, Sergeant, Dec. 22, 1863, to Sept. 3, 1865.
Orin H. Belcher, Corporal, Dec. 22, 1863, to Sept. 3, 1865.
Horatio W. Cole, Corporal, Dec. 22, 1863, to Sept. 3, 1865.
Henry B. Dyer, Dec. 22, 1863, to June 22, 1865.
Jacob A. Dyer, Dec. 22, 1863, to Sept. 3, 1865.
Henry Joy, Dec. 22, 1863, to May 26, 1865.

3d Heavy Artillery. Co. D.

Lewis Hobart, March 30, 1864. Deserted Aug. 23, 1865.

Co. E.

John Cronin, Corporal, Aug. 27, 1863, to Sept 18, 1865.
Patrick Regan, Aug. 27, 1863. Deserted Aug. 4, 1865.

Co. F.

Edward H. Mellus, Sergeant, Sept. 16, 1863; 2d Lieutenant, May 28, 1864.
Shubael M. Norton, Sept. 16, 1863, to Sept. 18, 1865.
Caleb S. Benson, Aug. 24, 1864; June 17, 1865.
William B. Denton, Sept. 24, 1864; June 17, 1865.
Lawrence A. Dyer, Sept. 16, 1863; Sept. 18, 1865.
Pearl S. Grindall, Sept. 16, 1863; Nov. 1, 1864.
Elias Holbrook, Aug. 24, 1864; June 20, 1865.
Chas. H. Howe, Aug. 23, 1864; June 20, 1865.
Hosea Jackson, Aug. 23, 1864; June 17, 1865.
Hervey N. Jillson, Aug. 24, 1864; June 17, 1865.
John G. Minchin, Aug. 23, 1864; June 17, 1865.
Martin V. B. Minchin, Aug. 23, 1864; June 17, 1865.
Henry O. Pratt, Sept. 16, 1863; Sept. 18, 1865.
Andrew J. Rupert, Aug. 24, 1864; June 17, 1865.
Samuel W. Savill, Aug. 24, 1864; June 17, 1865.

Co. G.

Eli W. Chase, Oct. 20, 1863; Sept. 18, 1865.
Robert M. Cummings, Oct. 20, 1863; Sept. 18, 1865.

Co. K.

Robert Rennie, Corporal, May 12, 1864; Sept. 18, 1865.

Co. L.

Charles F. Arnold, Corporal, Aug. 29, 1864; June 17, 1865.
Amos W. Hobart, Artificer, Aug. 29, 1865; June 17, 1865.
Cyrus G. Bowker, Aug. 29, 1864; June 17, 1865.
Alfred H. Butler, Aug. 29, 1864; June 17, 1865.
Elbridge Joy, Aug. 29, 1864; June 17, 1865.
Joseph P. Thayer, Aug. 29, 1864; June 17, 1865.

4th Heavy Artillery. Co. C.

Orace W. Allen, Sergeant, Aug. 9, 1864; June 17, 1865.
Nahum Sampson, Sergeant, Aug. 15, 1864; May 5, 1865.
Wm. C. Stoddard, Corporal, Aug. 9, 1864; June 17, 1865.
Cyrus Cummings, Wagoner, Aug. 13, 1864; June 17, 1865.
John G. N. Henderson, Aug. 10, 1864; June 17, 1865.
Lothrop C. Keith, Aug. 9, 1864; June 17, 1865.
William C. Knight, Aug. 11, 1864; June 17, 1865.
John Laing, Aug. 12, 1864; June 17, 1865.
Angus McGilvray, Aug. 10, 1864; June 17, 1865.
Michael Nugent, Aug. 10, 1864; June 17, 1865.

Co. F.

John Flynn, Aug. 15, 1864, to June 17, 1865.

Co. G.

Robert T. Bestick, Aug. 26, 1864; June 17, 1865.
George C. H. Deets, Aug. 26, 1864; June 17, 1865.
Samuel B. Holbrook, Aug. 26, 1864; June 17, 1865.
James Toole, Aug. 26, 1864; June 17, 1865.

Co. K.

William M. Strachan, 1st Sergeant, Aug. 18, 1864; 2d Lieutenant (Boston), Feb. 19, 1865, to June 17, 1865.

1st Battalion Heavy Artillery. Co. A.

Benjamin J. Loring, Jr., 1st Sergeant, Feb. 26, 1862; Feb. 27, 1865.
George S. Huff, Sergeant, Feb. 26, 1862; Feb. 27, 1865.
Charles E. Pratt, Corporal, Feb. 21, 1862; Feb. 27, 1865.
Henry Bayley, July 1, 1864; June 22, 1865.
Frank Osborn, Feb. 24, 1862; July 20, 1862.
Elihu M. Thayer, Feb. 19, 1862. Re-enlisted, March 1, 1864, to Oct. 20, 1865.

Co. B.

Calvin T. Dyer, Sept. 10, 1863; June 29, 1865.
John Q. Ela, Dec. 3, 1863; June 29, 1865.
Edward A. Hale, Oct. 29, 1862; June 29, 1865.
George B. Jones, Oct. 29, 1862; June 29, 1865.
~~Charles M. Keating, Oct. 30, 1862. Accidentally shot Oct. 31, 1862.~~ *See p 44.*
Michael B. McCormick, Jan. 13, 1863; June 29, 1865.
George H. Randall, Aug. 7, 1863; June 29, 1865.
Wilbert F. Robbins, Dec. 4, 1863; June 29, 1865.
William H. Saunders, Oct. 25, 1862; June 29, 1865.
Jacob C. Snow, Aug. 18, 1863; June 29, 1865.
Benj. F. Spear, Aug. 7, 1863; June 29, 1865.

Co. C.

Francis White, Quartermaster-Sergeant, Aug. 22, 1863; Oct. 20, 1865.
Warren C. Mansfield, Aug. 3, 1863; June 29, 1865.
William H. McQuinn, Aug. 18, 1862; June 29, 1865.
Samuel E. Whitmarsh, April 22, 1863; Oct. 20, 1865.

Co. D.

Charles Blake, June 6, 1863. *Deserted,* May 31, 1864.

1st Cavalry. Co. H.

Peter A. Drollett, Oct. 12, 1861, to Oct. 8, 1864.
Alvin Jackson, Oct. 12, 1861, to Jan. 10, 1863. Re-enlisted 4th Cavalry.

Co. K.

William A. Daggett, Bugler, Sept. 17, 1861. Transferred to 4th Cavalry.
James B. Frazier, Nov. 26, 1861. Transferred to 4th Cavalry.
Henry A. Hobart, Nov. 26, 1861. Transferred to 4th Cavalry.
George F. Penniman, Sept. 25, 1861. Transferred to 4th Cavalry.

See p 44.

2d Cavalry. Co. F.

Henry W. Gammons, Jan. 2, 1865, to July 20, 1865.
George F. Thayer, April 3, 1863. Killed April 1, 1865.

Co. H.

Owen Fox, Oct. 9, 1863. Killed July 6, 1864.

3d Cavalry. Co. B.

Edwin L. Curtis, Sergeant, Dec. 11, 1863, to Sept. 28, 1865.

Co. D.

Richard M. Sanborn, 1st Sergeant, Jan. 30, 1864; 2d Lieutenant, Aug. 17, 1865.
Theodore C Howe. Q. M. Sergeant, Dec. 7, 1863; 1st Lieutenant, Oct. 5, 1865.
Hosea B. Hayden, Corporal, Dec. 31, 1863, to Sept 28, 1865.
Wm. G. Hill, Corporal, Dec. 5, 1863, to July 29, 1865.
Joseph W. Huff, Corporal, March 11, 1864, to Sept. 28, 1865.
Charles B. Leonard, Corporal, Dec. 21, 1863, to Sept. 28, 1865.
Jonathan R Clark, Blacksmith, Dec. 31, 1863, to Sept 28, 1865
George V. Chick, Dec. 5, 1863, to Sept. 28, 1865.
Stephen W. Dawson, Jan. 29, 1864. Died (Belonged in Taunton.)
John Halpin, Dec. 28, 1863, to Sept. 28, 1865.
Isaac R. Harmon, Feb. 15, 1864, to Sept 28, 1865.
Philip McQuinty, Jan. 5, 1864, to July 29, 1865.
George A. Mower, Feb. 9, 1864, to Sept. 28, 1865.
James Spear, Dec. 10, 1863, to Sept. 28, 1865.
Charles S. Thayer, Feb. 15, 1864, to Aug. 19, 1865.

Co. E.

James Riley, Sept. 20, 1862. *Deserted* Nov. 25, 1862.

Co. G.

Patrick Dunlay, Nov. 1, 1862, to May 20, 1865.

Co. I.

Royal Belcher, Aug. 5 1862, to May 20, 1865.
James Smith, Aug. 5, 1862, to May 20, 1865.

Co. K.

John T. Ayres, 1st Sergeant, Aug 6, 1862. Killed Oct. 19, 1864, at Cedar Creek, Va.
Timothy Curran, Corporal, Aug. 6,

1862. Transferred, Aug. 20, 1864, to Veteran Reserve Corps.
John G. Ingraham, Corporal, Aug 6, 1862, to March 1, 1863.
Jonathan S. Paine, Corporal, Aug 6, 1862. Transferred, Aug 20, 1863, to Veteran Reserve Corps.
Wm A. Bishop, Bugler, Aug. 6, 1862, to May 30, 1865
Edward E. Patten, Saddler, Aug. 6, 1862. Died of wounds, Nov. 15, 1864.
John F. Albee, Feb 29, 1864. Died June 22, 1864.
Edward Bannon, Aug. 6, 1862; May 21, 1865.
John Barry, Aug. 6, 1862; Sept. 28, 1865.
Lewis D. Bates, Aug. 6, 1862; May 21, 1865.
Leonard Belcher, Aug. 6, 1862; March 1, 1863.
Elisha S. Bowditch, Dec 7, 1863. Died Sept 19, 1864.
James E. Burpee, Aug. 6, 1862 Transferred to Veteran Reserve Corps, Aug 20, 1864.
Patrick Cahill, Dec. 12, 1863, to July 5, 1865.
Stephen Connor, Aug 6, 1862, to May 21, 1865.
Chandler Cox, Aug. 6, 1862, to May 21, 1865.
Marcus Cram, Aug. 6, 1862; Jan. 26, 1864.
Wm. L. Cram. Aug. 6, 1864. *Deserted* March 1, 1863.
John Creddock, Aug. 6, 1862; May 21, 1865
Birdsey Curtis, Aug. 6, 1862. Absent.
Charles C. Davis, Aug. 6, 1862; Jan. 23, 1863
Joseph Dissotelle, Aug. 6, 1862; May 21, 1865
John Flood, Aug. 6, 1862; May 21, 1865.
Chas. E. Fogg, Aug 6, 1862; Aug. 9, 1865.
Wm. H. French, Aug. 6, 1862; May 21, 1865.
Thomas C. Gardner, Aug. 6, 1862; May 21, 1865.
Peter T. Godfrey, Aug. 6, 1862. *Deserted.*
Oliver S. Harrington, Aug. 6, 1862, to May 21, 1865.
Almond E. Ingalls, Dec. 21, 1863. Transferred to Veteran Reserve Corps, Jan. 17, 1865.
George A. Joy, Aug. 6, 1862, to April 27, 1863.
James Kennedy, Jan. 4, 1864. Transferred to Veteran Reserve Corps, Feb. 16, 1865.
Wm. S. Leach, Aug. 6, 1862. Died Aug. 7, 1863.
Frederick Marr, Aug. 6, 1862.

Wm. P. Martin, Feb. 22, 1864. Transferred to Veteran Reserve Corps.
Frank McConnetty, Aug. 6, 1862. Absent.
Michael McMurphy, Aug. 6, 1862. *Deserted* Dec. 8, 1862.
Wm. W. Mower, Dec. 21, 1863. *Deserted* Aug. 14, 1864.
Albert S. Nason, Aug. 6, 1862, to May 21, 1865.
Daniel W. Niles, Aug. 6, 1862, to May 21, 1865.
Samuel H. Paine, Aug. 6, 1862, to May 21, 1865.
Charles E. Pratt, Aug. 6, 1862, to Nov. 15, 1863.
Isaac Raymond, Aug. 6, 1862, to May 21, 1865.
Oliver Simmons, Aug. 6, 1862, to Feb. 18, 1863.
Quincy Sprague, Aug. 6, 1862, to May 21, 1865.
George H. Stevens, Dec. 21, 1863. Transferred to Veteran Reserve Corps, Dec. 20, 1864.
Ansel P. Thayer, Aug 6, 1862. Killed Sept. 19, 1864.
Ephraim F. Thayer, Dec. 31, 1863, to Aug. 8, 1865.
Major Tirrell, Aug. 6, 1862, to May 21, 1865.
Americus V. Tirrell, Aug. 6, 1862, to Jan. 14, 1864.
John F Wild, Dec. 26, 1863. Killed April 8, 1864.
Thomas S. Williams, Dec. 5, 1863. Transferred to Veteran Reserve Corps, Jan. 10, 1865.

Co. M.

Garrett G. Barry, Sergeant, Dec. 13, 1861. Re-enlisted Feb. 1, 1864. Killed April 8, 1864.

Rejected Recruit; not assigned to a Company.

Edward A. May, Feb. 18, 1864, to March 10, 1864.

Fourth Cavalry. Co. D.

Alvin Jackson, Jan. 9, 1864. Killed Jan. 15, 1865.

Co. F.

William L. Craw, Jan. 27, 1864, to Nov. 14, 1865.

Co. K.

Henry A. Hobart, Sergeant, Nov. 26, 1861. 1st Cavalry. (Re-enlisted, April 10, 1864.) *Deserted* Aug. 9, 1865. (See 1st Cavalry.)
William A Daggett, Bugler, Sept. 17, 1861, to Sept. 21, 1864. (See 1st Cavalry.)

James B. Frazier, Nov. 6, 1861, to Jan. 4, 1865. (See 1st Cavalry.)
George F. Penniman, Sept. 25, 1861, to Sept. 25, 1864. (See 1st Cavalry.)

5th Cavalry.

James M. Cutting, Veterinary Surgeon, Sept. 16, 1864, to Oct. 31, 1865.

2d Infantry. Co. G.

William Foley, May 25, 1861, to July 26, 1863
Dennis Moriarty, May 25, 1861. Died, April 1, 1862. (Boston)
William Welsh, May 25, 1861, to Jan. 31, 1863.

9th Infantry. Co. B.

John Healey, June 11, 1861. *Deserted* Sept. 22, 1861.

Co. C.

John P. Murphy, June 11, 1861, to June 21, 1864.

Co. G.

Cornelius Furfy, June 11, 1861. Killed July 1, 1862.
Richard Furfy, June 11, 1861, to June 21, 1864.

Co. H.

John Foley, Aug. 21, 1863. Transferred June 10, 1864, to 32d Regiment.

Co. K.

Anthony Columbus, Aug. 21, 1863. Transferred, June 10, 1864, to 32d Regiment.

11th Infantry. Co. B.

John P. Maloney, Sergeant, June 13, 1861. *Deserted* Nov. 15, 1861.
William M. Tirrell, Sergeant, June 13, 1861, to June 24, 1864.
James Wilkie, Corporal, June 13, 1861. *Deserted* April 29, 1862.

Co. D.

Owen Greenlish, June 13, 1861, to Aug. 22, 1861.

Co. E.

Francis Marmont, Aug. 14, 1863, to July 14, 1865.

Co. K.

James Barrett, June 13, 1861. *Deserted* May 15, 1862.
Thomas H. Neal, June 13, 1861, to Oct. 22, 1862.
Samuel W. Saville, June 13, 1861, to June 24, 1864.
Thomas Wilson, Aug. 12, 1863, to July 14, 1865.

12th Infantry. Co. C.

Francis W. Kahle, July 22, 1863. Died March 6, 1864.
Michael Preston, July 5, 1861, to Dec. 31, 1862.
Ephraim F. Thayer, June 26, 1861, to Feb. 28, 1863.
John Q. Whitmarsh, June 26, 1861. Died Sept. 18, 1862. (Weymouth.)

Co. E.

Christopher P. Tower, June 26, 1861, to March 9, 1863.

Co. F.

Joseph P. Davis, June 26, 1861, to July 8, 1864.

Co. H.

Charles A. Pope, 1st Sergeant, June 26, 1861. Died Nov. 30, 1863. (Enlisted in Weymouth.)
Warren Stetson, July 17, 1863. Transferred, June 25, 1864, to 39th.
John Q. A. Thayer, June 26, 1861, to July 8, 1864.

13th Infantry. Co. G.

Hiram S. Thayer, July 16, 1861, to Aug. 1, 1864.

16th Infantry. Co. I.

William Cunningham, Aug. 30, 1861, to July 15, 1865

Co. K.

James Bradley, July 2, 1861, to July 27, 1864. (From Waltham, in State record.)

17th Infantry. Co. E.

Albert T. Poole, Sept. 5, 1864, to June 30, 1865.
John F. Poole, Sept. 5, 1864, to June 30, 1865.

Co. G.

John Navan, Aug. 29, 1864, to June 30, 1865.

18th Infantry. Co. E.

Asa W. Holbrook, Aug. 24, 1861. Re-enlisted, Jan. 1, 1864. Transferred, Oct. 26, 1864, to 32d Infantry.

Co. K.

Thomas Smith, Jr, Corporal, Aug. 24, 1861, to Jan. 26, 1863.

19th Infantry. Co. B.

Duncan Crawford, Aug. 3, 1863. Transferred, Jan. 14, 1864, to 20th.

Co. E.

Daniel Corrigan, Sergeant, Sept. 2, 1861. Re-enlisted, Dec. 22, 1863, to June 30, 1865.
James Carrigan, July 26, 1861. Re-enlisted, Dec. 22, 1863, Veteran Reserve Corps.

Co. K.

Samuel D. Chase, Corporal, Oct. 31, 1862, to June 30, 1865.
Marcus P. Arnold, Oct. 29, 1862. Re-enlisted, Feb. 16, 1864, to June 30, 1865.
(Unassigned. N. A. White, Aug. 19, 1861. No record of discharge.)

20th Infantry. Co. E.

Horatio N. Faxon, Aug. 15, 1862. Killed at Antietam, Sept. 17, 1862. (Accredited to Quincy.)

Co. F.

Duncan Crawford, Jan. 14,1864. Transferred to navy, April 23, 1864.

Co. G.

John Goodman, Sept. 4, 1861, to Sept. 3, 1864.

Co. I.

Charles Holbrook, Dec. 9, 1861, to Oct. 15, 1862.

Co. K.

Thomas J. Crowell, Corporal, Aug. 21, 1861. Killed Dec. 13, 1862.

22d Infantry. Co. E.

Jeremiah Dalton, 2d, Corporal, Oct. 1, 1861. Killed June 27, 1862.

Co. F.

Charles L. Holbrook, July 28, 1863. Transferred, Oct. 26, 1864, to 32d.
Edward Huff, July 17, 1863. Transferred, Oct. 26, 1864, to 32d.

Co. I.

Charles H. Crickmay, Corporal, Sept. 6, 1861. Died of wounds, June 30, 1862.
Alexander R. Fogg, Sept. 6, 1861. Killed June 27, 1862.

23d Infantry. Co. H.

George B. Jones, Sept. 28, 1861, to Sept. 8, 1862.

24th Infantry. Co. B.

George White, Sept. 18, 1861. Re-enlisted, Dec. 18, 1863, for Quincy.

Co. C.

Daniel Austin Thayer, July 29, 1862. Died Jan. 4, 1864.

Co. G.

Loring N. Hayden, Corporal, Nov. 15, 1861. Re-enlisted, Jan. 3, 1864, to Jan. 20, 1866.
Edward M. French, Nov. 13, 1861, to Aug. 4, 1863.
W. Martin Harmon, Nov. 13, 1861. Died April 30, 1863.
Abraham W. Hobart, July 26, 1862. Re-enlisted, Jan. 4, 1864. *Deserted* Aug. 17, 1865.
Seth Taunt, Dec. 5, 1861. Re-enlisted, Jan. 4, 1864, to July 15, 1865.
George N. Thayer, Sept. 16, 1861. Re-enlisted, Jan. 4, 1864, to Jan. 20, 1866.

Co. H.

James L. Curtis, July 29, 1862. Re-enlisted for Randolph, Jan. 4, 1864, to Jan. 20, 1866.

27th Infantry. Co. D.

Maxon G. Healey, July 23, 1862, to Sept. 27, 1864.

28th Infantry. Co. B.

John Connors, Aug. 10, 1863. Died July 6, 1864.
Amos A. Loring, Jan. 5, 1864. Died at City Point, Va.

Co. C.

Henry Barton, Dec. 13, 1861, to Dec. 19, 1864.

Co. D.

John Connor, Sergeant, Jan. 2, 1864; 1st Lieutenant (Boston), Aug. 19, 1864.
Adams H. Cogswell, Jan. 2, 1862.
Charles Gray, Aug. 10, 1863. Died Sept. 15, 1864.
William Reevers, Aug. 12, 1863, to June 20, 1865.

Co. F.

Thomas Smith, Jan. 8, 1862, to Sept. 30, 1862.

Co. G.

Charles Miller, Aug. 12, 1863. *Deserted* Aug. 31, 1863.
Francis Winn, Dec. 19, 1861. *Deserted* June 29, 1863.

Co. I.

Frederick Smith, Aug. 11, 1863. *Deserted.*

Unassigned Recruit.

Peter Higgins, Aug. 14, 1863.

29th Infantry. Co. A.

John W. Sweeney, May 21, 1861, to Aug. 28, 1862.

Co. B.

Ira D. Bryant, May 14, 1861.
James Freel, May 14, 1861.
George S. Whiting; no record.

Co. D.

John Conley, Aug. 20, 1864, to July 29, 1865.
James Flinn, Aug. 19, 1864. *Deserted* Jan. 19, 1865.

30th Infantry. Co. F.

Samuel F. Harrington, Nov. 18, 1861. Re-enlisted, Jan. 2, 1864, to July 5, 1866.

31st Infantry. Co. K.

Ebenezer C. Thayer, Jr., Corporal, Jan. 29, 1862; June 25, 1863, 2d Lieutenant, 2d La.
John W. Dargan, Jan. 23, 1862. Signal Corps, Nov. 27, 1864.
Wm. Kayhoo, Jan. 17, 1862, to Feb. 14, 1864; to re-enlist.
John Rennie, Feb. 6, 1862, to Nov. 1, 1862.

32d Infantry. Co. E.

Loring W. Thayer, 1st Sergeant, Dec. 2, 1861. Re-enlisted Jan. 5, 1864. Killed Sept. 30, 1864.
Norman F. Steele, 1st Sergeant, Dec. 2, 1861; 2d Lieutenant.
James B. Leonard, Corporal, Dec. 2, 1861; 2d Lieutenant.
Leonard F. Huff, Dec. 2, 1861. Died Aug. 23, 1862.
Henry T. Wade, Dec. 2, 1861. Killed July 2, 1863.

Co. F.

Asa W. Holbrook, Jan. 21, 1864, to June 29, 1865.

Co. H.

John Foley, Aug. 21, 1863, to June 29, 1865.

Co. I.

Wm. Daley, Musician, Aug. 11, 1862. Re-enlisted, Jan. 4, 1864, to June 29, 1865.
Anthony Columbus, Aug. 22, 1863. Died.

Co. L.

Charles L. Holbrook, July 28, 1863, to June 29, 1865.
Edward Huff, July 17, 1863, to June 29, 1865.

33d *Infantry.* Co. E.

Edgar L. Bumpus, Sergeant, Aug. 5, 1862. (See Com. Officers.) Killed May 15, 1864.

Co. K.

Martin Branley, Aug. 8, 1862, to Nov. 24, 1862.
T. Horace Cain, Aug. 8, 1862. Died July 7, 1865.
Wm. Mulligan, Aug. 8, 1862, to June 11, 1865.
John W. W. Rowell, Aug. 8, 1862, to Dec. 28, 1863.
James N. Tower, Aug. 8, 1862, to June 11, 1865.
Nathaniel A. White, Aug. 8, 1862. Transferred to Veteran Reserve Corps, May 2, 1864.

35th *Infantry.* Co. E.

Wm. D. Lyons, Aug. 19, 1862, to April 20, 1863.

Co. H.

John Davis, Aug. 19, 1862. Died Aug. 23, 1863. (Enlisted in Weymouth.)

Chas. H. Loring. Serg^t Aug 19.62 to June 9 . 65

36th *Infantry.* Co. K.

Albert G. Wilder, Corporal Aug. 11, 1862. Transferred to Veteran Reserve Corps, May 31, 1864.
Daniel W. Dean, Aug 8, 1862. Died.
Seth Dean, Aug. 8, 1862. Died Jan. 27, 1863.

38th *Infantry.* Co. I.

Edward Freel, Aug. 21, 1862, to Feb. 14, 1863.
John V. Hunt, Aug. 21, 1862, to June 30, 1865.
James W. Thayer, Aug 21, 1862. Veteran Reserve Corps, May 31, 1864.
Stephen Thayer, Aug. 21, 1862, to June 30, 1865.

Co. K.

Hiram P. Abbott, Corporal, Aug. 20, 1862, to June 30, 1865.
Henry H. Shedd, Corporal, Aug. 20, 1862, to Oct. 24, 1862.
George H. Bryant, Aug. 20, 1862, to March 24, 1863.
Warren R. Dalton, Aug. 20, 1862, to June 30, 1865.
Charles David, Aug. 20, 1862, to Feb. 13, 1863.
Edward David, Aug. 20, 1862. Killed June 14, 1863.
Solon David, Aug. 20, 1862, to June 30, 1865.

39th *Infantry.* Co. G.

James Bannon, Sept. 2, 1862. Died April 12, 1865.
Warren Stetson, July 17, 1863, to May 18, 1865.

Co. H.

John Preston, Sept. 2, 1862, to Jan. 29, 1863.

40th *Infantry.* Co. F.

Michael McMurphy, Sept. 3, 1862, to March 24, 1863.

Co. H.

Daniel F. Leonard, Sept. 1. 1862, to Veteran Reserve Corps, March 15, 1865.

56th *Infantry.* Co. E.

Michael P. Foley, Jan. 12, 1864, to July 12, 1865.

58th *Infantry.* Co. E.

Joseph Jenkins, March 1, 1864, to July 14, 1865.

1st Co. Sharp-Shooters.

Josiah H. Hunt, Oct. 31, 1862. Veteran Reserve Corps, March 16, 1864.
N. W. Penniman, Oct. 13, 1862. Re-enlisted, Feb. 16, 1864, to July 25, 1864.

Veteran Reserve Corps.

Wm. Butler, Sept. 3, 1864.
Patrick Calahan, May 16, 1864.
Barney Feeney, May 16, 1864.
Peter Hutchbeck, May 17, 1864.
Edward Kellogg, May 17, 1864.
Jethro Lynch, May 16, 1864.
Jesse B. Nourse, April 11, 1864.

UNITED STATES SERVICE, REGULAR ARMY AND VOLUNTEERS.

Albert F. Wood, 1st U. S. Artillery, from April 11, 1861, to April 11, 1864.

Musicians.

Abijah Allen, enlisted Dec. 22, 1863. Band of 2d Brigade, 1st Division, 2d Corps, Army of the Potomac. Discharged May 31, 1865.
Hiram A. French, enlisted Dec. 22, 1863. 1st Brigade, 1st Division, 2d Corps. Discharged May 31, 1865.
Eugene D. Daniels, enlisted Dec. 22, 1863. 1st Brigade, 1st Division, 2d Corps. Discharged May 31, 1865.

Luther Hayden, from Oct. 26, 1864, to June 13, 1865.
Francis W. Holbrook, from Jan. 4, 1864, to May 31, 1865. 1st Brigade, 1st Division, 2d Corps.
Jacob S. Lord, from Oct. 26, 1864, to June 13, 1865.
Jonathan Thayer, Jr., from Oct. 26, 1864, to June 13, 1865. Band, 3d Brigade, 1st Division, 20th Corps, Sherman's army.

70th Infantry (Colored).

John Bell, from Jan. 31, 1865, to

OTHER STATE ORGANIZATIONS.

70th N. Y. Infantry.

Levi Bunker, enlisted June 20, 1861. Died June 16, 1863.
Edward S. Bunker, enlisted July 13, 1861. Died Sept. 11, 1862.
Alfred E. Parker, enlisted July 15, 1861. Killed May 5, 1862.

25th N. Y. Infantry.

Thomas Smith, enlisted May 13, 1861. Died June —, 1862.

3d Maryland.

John Finnegan, enlisted Feb. —, 1862. Died March 12, 1863.
Alonzo A. Tower, enlisted Feb , 1862.

12th Vermont.

Benjamin F. Arnold, Oct 4, 1862, to July 21, 1863. Re-enlisted in 8th Vermont, Jan. 6, 1864. Died Dec. 29, 1864.
Nelson Arnold, Oct. 18, 1862, to July 21, 1863. Re-enlisted, 17th Vermont. Sept 29, 1863, to June 19, 1864 Killed.

Of Unknown Organizations.

William S. Adams.
William C. Bright.
Symes G. Baker.
James Dooley.
Michael Doran.
Edward Doyle.
Daniel B Ellis.
John Freel (2d enlistment).
James Flynn.
Patrick Glancy.
James T. Godfrey.
John Hanlon.
Albert Howard, Jr.
Lewis U Hubbard.
John W Langley.
Bernard McGovern.
George E. Nelson.
John O'Neil.
John Smith.
Charles E Smith.
William Taylor.
Edward Tilden.
William Townsend.
Peter Whitmarsh.
William O. Wright.

NAVY.

(A portion of these names were assigned to the town quota from the State at large. The correctness of many of them is uncertain.)

John Teried, enlisted Feb 19, 1862.
David H. Thayer, Jan. 18, 1862.
George Sheppard, July 10, 1862.
George Steechfield, July 15, 1862.
William Thompson, July 10, 1862.
George Thompson, July 8, 1862.
Charles Thompson, July 10, 1862.
John Thompson, July 12, 1862.
Michael Tenney, July 9, 1862.
James Tunneman, July 11, 1862.
John Smith, July 17, 1862.
Alexander B. Shaw, July 17, 1862.
Peter Shields, July 19, 1862.
Michael Staffer, July 15, 1862.
Dexter P. Moulton, Dec. 10, 1863.
Martin Murphy, Dec. 11, 1863.
James McLaughlin, Dec. 7, 1863.
Charles Marson, Dec 14, 1863.
Edward McCrady, Dec. 12, 1863.
Archibald McVane, Dec. 15, 1863.
Daniel Mullen, Dec. 16, 1863.
Patrick McCarthy, Dec. 15, 1863.

William McLaughlin, Dec. 18, 1863.
Lawrence McGuire, Dec. 17, 1863.
Patrick McCarthy, Dec. 18, 1863.
Patrick McWilliams, Dec. 18, 1863.
George E. Nelson, Aug 13, 1864.
Allan McDonald, Aug. 15, 1864.
Duncan Crawford, April 23, 1864.
Royal J. Freeman.
George Howe.
Thomas J. Martin.
George A Raymond.
William H. Spear.
Stephen Martin.
George R Horne.
Thomas Monahan.
Charles McDonald.
John McDonald.
John Newson.
James Nettleton.
Charles Smith.
Paul Nadell
William H. Mathews.

THE DEPARTMENTS IN WHICH THE FOREGOING REGIMENTS SERVED.

First Heavy Artillery, in the Army of the Potomac.
Second Heavy Artillery, in North Carolina (chiefly).
Third Heavy Artillery, in the defences of Boston Harbor and Washington.
Fourth Heavy Artillery, in the defences of Washington.
First Battalion, Heavy Artillery, in the forts of Boston Harbor, New Bedford, and Lake Champlain.
First Cavalry, in South Carolina, and in the Army of the Potomac.
Second Cavalry, in the Army of the Potomac.
Third Cavalry, in the Department of the Gulf, and Shenandoah Valley.
Fourth Cavalry, a part in South Carolina, and a part in the Army of the Potomac.
Fifth Cavalry, Army of the Potomac, and Gulf Department.
Second Infantry, Army of the Potomac, Army of the Cumberland, Sherman's march through Georgia and South Carolina.
Ninth Infantry, Army of the Potomac.
Eleventh Infantry, Army of the Potomac.
Twelfth Infantry, Army of the Potomac.
Thirteenth Infantry, Army of the Potomac.
Sixteenth Infantry, Army of the Potomac.
Seventeenth Infantry, Army of the Potomac.
Eighteenth Infantry, Army of the Potomac.
Twentieth Infantry, Army of the Potomac
Twenty-Second Infantry, Army of the Potomac.
Twenty-Third Infantry, in North Carolina.
Twenty-Fourth Infantry, in North Carolina and Army of Potomac.
Twenty-Seventh Infantry, in the Department of the South (South Carolina)
Twenty-Eighth Infantry, in the Department of the South and Army of the Potomac.

Twenty-Ninth Infantry, Army of the Potomac, of Mississippi and East Tennessee.
Thirtieth Infantry, Gulf Department (Louisiana).
Thirty-First Infantry, Gulf Department.
Thirty-Second Infantry, Army of the Potomac.
Thirty-Third Infantry, Army of the Potomac, of the Cumberland, and Sherman's march through Georgia and South Carolina.
Thirty-Fifth Infantry, Army of the Potomac.
Thirth-Sixth Infantry, Army of the Potomac and East Tennessee.
Thirty-Eighth Infantry, Gulf Department, Shenandoah Valley, and North Carolina.
Thirty-Ninth Infantry, Army of the Potomac.
Fortieth Infantry, Army of the Potomac.
Fifty-Fifth Infantry, Department of the South (South Carolina).
Fifty-Sixth Infantry, Army of the Potomac.
Fifty-Eighth Infantry, Army of the Potomac
Company of Sharp-Shooters, Army of the Potomac.
Twenty-Fifth and Seventieth New York, Third Maryland, Twelfth and Seventeenth Vermont, in the Army of the Potomac.
Second Louisiana, in the Gulf Department.
Fourth Militia, Fortress Monroe.
Fifth Militia, in Washington and at Bull Run.
Forty-Second Militia (100 days), in Washington.
Forty-Third Militia, in North Carolina.
Forty-Fourth Militia, in North Carolina.
Forty-Fifth Militia, in North Carolina.
Forty-Seventh Militia, in Louisiana.
Forty-Eighth Militia, in Louisiana.
Veteran Reserve Corps, in various defences of cities.
First United States Artillery, in the Army of the Potomac.

APPENDIX II.

An Account of the Services of Dedication of the Soldiers' Monument.

On the 17th of June, 1874, the monument erected in memory of the soldiers of Braintree who had died in service was dedicated with becoming formalities. Extended preparations had been made to give the occasion high distinction among the festival days of the town, and although occasional showers somewhat interfered with the full success of the arranged programme of services, yet in all respects the ceremonies were thoroughly impressive and enjoyable. The houses and grounds of citizens and the public buildings were elaborately decorated, and the principal streets were crowded with visitors, among the invited guests being His Excellency Governor Talbot and his council.

The arrangements of the procession were carried out creditably by Capt. James T. Stevens, the chief marshal of the day. The procession formed at the Town House at about nine o'clock in the forenoon, led by the organization of old soldiers of the town, Gen. Sylvanus Thayer Post, 87, Grand Army of the Republic, which was followed by visiting Posts from Randolph, Quincy, Weymouth, and South Boston, by several Masonic bodies, and by invited guests and prominent citizens in carriages. Marching through the main street of the town, it was dismissed at noon for dinner in a large tent raised on the Common, and in the Town House.

At two o'clock, P. M., the unveiling of the monument, which stands upon the town grounds, near the Town House and public library, was performed in the following order: —

MUSIC BY THE BRAINTREE BRASS BAND.

READING OF THE REPORT OF THE SOLDIERS' MONUMENT COMMITTEE,

BY F. A. HOBART, AS FOLLOWS:

The committee appointed by the citizens, and subsequently authorized by the town, to erect a suitable memorial to the men of Braintree who died or were killed in service during the war of the Rebellion, having concluded their labors, respectfully submit their report.

Early in the year 1865, before peace had been declared and the war of the Rebellion ended, a meeting of the citizens of Braintree was held in the Town Hall, to devise measures to secure the erection of a suitable memorial to the soldiers, from the town, who died or were killed in service.

This meeting was very fully attended, and the unanimous expression of opinion was favorable to the object.

At this meeting a committee, consisting of Messrs. F. A. Hobart, Asa French, Horace Abercrombie, Levi W. Hobart, and E. W. Arnold, was appointed to take the matter into consideration, with instructions to take such preliminary action as they might deem advisable to secure the necessary funds for the erection of a monument. This committee, after consultation, finding that there was a general willingness on the part of all our people to do something in aid of the object, decided to hold a fair and levee at Town Hall, and invited the ladies to co-operate with them in making the necessary arrangements therefor.

To this invitation a ready and liberal response was made, and a fair subsequently held, the net proceeds of which realized a little upwards of thirteen hundred dollars ($1,300).

This sum was afterwards increased to about fourteen hundred dollars, by means of a musical entertainment given by the young folks. The fund thus raised was loaned by the committee to the town.

No further action was taken until March, 1867, when the matter was brought to the attention of the town by the committee, an article being inserted in the warrant, "to see if the town will make an appropriation in aid of the erection of a soldiers' monument, and authorize the committee to procure plans and estimates."

At that meeting the committee previously selected by the citizens was adopted by the town, and Jason G. Howard, Edward Avery, Alva Morrison, and Edward Potter added thereto. It was also voted, "that the Committee on the Soldiers' Monument be authorized to procure plans and estimates, and report the result, for future action by the town."

Several meetings of the committee were subsequently held, but for various reasons no definite conclusions were reached.

On the 4th of March, 1872, the committee, feeling that it was time that some progress was made and something definite done, made a partial report to the town. The matter was fully discussed, but owing to a diversity of opinion manifest as to what form the memorial should take, no course of action was adopted. At this meeting, however, it was voted, "That the town sell the lot of land adjoining the town lands, known as the School House Lot, at public auction, the proceeds of the sale to be appropriated to the use of the Soldiers' Monument Committee.

At the annual meeting, March 3, 1873, the subject was further discussed by the town, and the opinion generally expressed that the work should be completed at an early day. At this meeting James T. Stevens and Wm. M. Richards were, by vote of the town, added to the committee to fill vacancies caused by the removal from town of Edward Potter and Jason G. Howard.

Subsequently several meetings were held and various plans suggested and discussed, there appearing a difference of opinion upon the form of memorial that should be adopted, a portion of the committee favoring the erection of a monumental shaft, while another portion advocated placing marble tablets in the Free Public Library Building, then in process of erection.

It was finally determined to submit the question to the decision of the town, and at a special meeting held on the twenty-seventh day of June, 1873, numerously attended, after a full and thorough discussion of the whole subject it was voted nearly unanimously "That the Soldiers' Monument Committee be instructed to erect upon some portion of the town land, near the Town House, a statue cut in granite, after a model submitted by Messrs. Batterson & Canfield, of Hartford, Conn., with a pedestal designed by Messrs. H. & J. E. Billings, architects, of Boston, at a cost not exceeding $5,000, above the foundation."

The committee, representing to the meeting that with the "Citizens, Fund," so called, and previous appropriations made by the town, the sum of $2,500 additional would be sufficient to complete the work, it was voted "That the sum of $2,500 be raised and appropriated, and the whole, or so much of the same as may be necessary, be placed at the disposal of the Soldiers' Monument Committee, for the erection of a monumental statue to our deceased soldiers, in accordance with a vote passed at this meeting, the said sum to be additional to any moneys already voted to be appropriated by the town for this purpose."

April 6, 1874, the town by vote appropriated $500 in addition to all previous appropriations, and authorized the committee to make the necessary arrangements for dedication.

By the will of Mr. Harvey White, also, recently admitted to probate, a generous legacy of $500 was given towards the erection of this monument, which has not yet been received, but which we have anticipated in the expenditures already incurred.

The committee, after consultation with competent judges, and by advice of the Messrs. Billings, whose skill and judgment as architects stand in the foremost rank, awarded the contract to Messrs. Batterson & Canfield, of Hartford, who, we are gratified to state, have performed their work in a thorough and satisfactory manner. The foundation is substantially constructed of granite, and was built by contract by Mr. N. M. Hobart of this town.

4

The statue is a full-sized model of a soldier, standing with his musket in position, *at rest*, and is cut from Westerly granite, which is considered by those best competent to judge equal if not superior to any other for this purpose.

Fortunately, no difference of opinion existed either on the part of the committee or among the citizens of the town upon the question of location, all conceding that it should be placed in the most honorable and conspicuous position, upon the town lands in close proximity to the public buildings of the town.

The committee have used every effort to secure an accurate and correct list of all who died or were killed in service, upon the quota of the town, and trust no errors have been committed.

The inscriptions placed upon the pedestal are, upon the front, " The town of Braintree builds this monument in grateful remembrance of the brave men whose names it bears "; also, " 1874," denoting the year of its erection. Upon the reverse this simple inscription, " Dying they triumphed."

Upon the north and south sides are the names of those of the quota of Braintree who died or were killed in service, and the regiments to which they belonged; also, " 1861" at the top and " 1865 " beneath, denoting the duration of the war.

The funds placed at the disposal of the committee were as follows : —

Citizens' fund and interest	.	. $2,338 19
Town appropriations . .	.	. 3,628 07
Due from legacy Harvey White	.	. 500 00
		$6,466 26

The expenditures have been, for

Foundation work, }		
Statue and pedestal,		
Grading, etc., } about		6,000 00
Plans,		
Incidental expenses, }		

Leaving for expenses of dedication and completion of grading, about $500 00

F. A. HOBART, Chairman.

Asa French,	James T. Stevens,
L. W. Hobart,	Alverdo Mason,
E. W. Arnold,	Wm. M. Richards,
Horace Abercrombie,	Marcus A. Perkins,
Alva Morrison,	C. W. Procter,
Abijah Allen,	

Monument Committee.

After the reading of this report, Mr. Hobart continued. —

Now, fellow-citizens, having concluded with the exercises of this day the duty you selected us to perform, your committee submit their report, and unveil to your view the result of their labors, surrendering into your hands and keeping forever the emblematic structure which we to-day dedicate to the memory of the men of Braintree who fell in the war of the Rebellion.

It is to the memory of her soldiers that the citizens of Braintree have raised this pedestal of solid granite, placing thereon this mute sentinel to watch over and guard their graves. No truer husbands, no fonder fathers, no kinder brothers, no more cherished sons ever faced the foe in the stern vicissitudes of conflict than the martyrs whose ashes repose beneath our soil or whose bones still bleach upon Southern battle-fields. Fresh in our recollection are the manly looks and the martial bearing of those men as they left our midst to engage in the fierce contest for national life. With pride we recall the feats of daring and courage, the unsubdued spirit, the soul unshaken by defeat, the sublime victories of that Grand Army in which our townsmen were numbered in the Roll of Honor; and well, oh! too well we remember, how, one by one, they came back to us silent in death, to be borne in sad and solemn procession through our streets to the spot of burial, their loss causing the gray head to bow with grief, and sending the burden of sorrow to the hearts of those who loved them, making forsaken firesides and desolate hearths in many of our homes.

Time has softened in some degree the cruel stroke that fell so heavily on mourning circles, and we reconcile ourselves to submission, because we know that to them and their living comrades we owe the uncounted blessings and the unspeakable privileges which we to-day enjoy as citizens.

Better or braver men never poured out their blood or yielded up their lives for the good of their native land; and as our children in the years hereafter shall gaze on this memorial offering, remembering the dust it hallows, the inward, unspoken thanksgiving shall go up to God that our old and honorable town had her full share of heroes, to do, to dare, and to die for the preservation of the Republic and the liberties of the people; and while the world stands, the pealing anthem, the solemn prayer, and this enduring memento shall perpetuate the remembrance of their gallant lives and their patriotic death.

At the close of this fitting address, prayer was made by Rev. George S. Ball, of Upton, Grand Chaplain of the Grand Army of Massachusetts, and after vocal music, the assemblage adjourned to Yale's large tent on the Common. Here, before an audience of several thousand people, the Rev. Louis E. Charpiot asked the blessing of God upon the day; a select chorus, led by N. Warren Penniman, sang Eichberg's hymn,

> "To thee, O country, great and free,
> With trusting hearts we cling,"

and the president of the afternoon, Asa French, gave the following address : —

Braintree at last renders tardy honor to the memory of its dead heroes. To-day we build a monument which proclaims to the world our undying gratitude and affection for the brave men whose names are inscribed upon it. And we fondly hope that it will endure for all time as a testimony to our children and our children's children that we were not unmindful of the debt we owe to them. How great a debt it is! How inadequate our payment! It seems but yesterday since they went out from among us, — those fathers and brothers, husbands and sons; with firm step and hearts that knew no fear, they went forth to defend with their lives that country which they and we loved so well. Our prayers and hopes went with them. Through many a weary march they toiled, on many a battle-field they fought: bravely and without complaint they toiled, bravely they fought, and died. On battle-field, in camp, in hospital, some, thank God, at home, surrounded and ministered to by loving friends, — they all died *for us!* But "dying they triumphed," — triumphed in the success of the cause for which they fell. Nay, even over death itself they triumphed, for in death they are immortal.

There are hearts that will bleed anew, and eyes that will fill with tears to-day as they read the names inscribed on yonder monument. The faces and forms of brothers and sons, long since buried out of sight, will come back again in memory, and grief will be felt as over new-made graves.

As we pay merited honor to the dead, let us not forget the living, who laid these, their most precious offerings, on the altar of their country. Nor shall our gratitude ever fail towards those who, braving the perils of war in the same cause for which their comrades died, were permitted to come back to their homes in health and strength. Justly we assign to them the post of honor on this occasion. The post of honor in our hearts they shall ever hold!

This day we consecrate to the precious dead. Our duty will be best performed if we forget ourselves and think only of them and their deeds. And as we dwell upon the simple but heroic story of their lives, may their example cause to grow in our hearts a deeper and purer love of country, and a stronger devotion to the principles for which their blood was shed.

Baldwin's Band, of Boston, played a dirge; Rev. George A. Thayer, of Boston, read the necrology which constitutes the principal part of this volume; other music by the chorus followed; and the orator of the day, Major-Gen. Nathaniel P. Banks, then gave an acceptable address, which, being wholly without notes, could not be adequately reported. After more vocal and instrumental music, the audience was dismissed with a benediction from Rev. S. P. Andrews.

APPENDIX III.

THE part taken by the women of the town in bearing the burdens of the war was too honorable to be left without notice.

Early in the fall of 1861 active efforts were made by the women at public gatherings to create an interest among their sex in contributing to the needs of the soldiers' hospitals, and as a result, creditable contributions were made to the Sanitary Commission, that grand and noble charitable organization which saved so many thousands of men's lives in the course of the war.

In the summer of 1862 these efforts took organized shape by the formation of a branch of the Sanitary Commission, of which Mrs. Daniel F. Leonard was chosen president, Miss Amelia L. Bumpus, secretary, and Miss Catharine Willis, treasurer.

This society never had any large sums of money at its disposal, but diligent hands made up many packages of bedding, clothing, lint and bandages, and delicacies of diet, which were gratefully acknowledged by the Sanitary Commission agents, and often heard from as ministering to many a needy sufferer in the army.

An illustration of the spirit of some of the women in raising funds for these purposes of mercy is worth preserving. One summer, when money was hard to get, a townsman jocosely offered, without thinking his proposal would be accepted, to give the ladies a load of hay, lying in the wet meadows, if they would carry it away. They promptly accepted the gift, and as men were not forward to offer their help without pay, several of the younger women went into the fields, loaded the hay, had it properly weighed, and duly deposited in the barn of a purchaser, and converted the proceeds into stockings, drawers, and shirts for the men at the front.

www.ingramcontent.com/pod-product-compliance
Lightning Source LLC
Chambersburg PA
CBHW031803090426
42739CB00008B/1143